The Trouble with Advertising . . .

*A partisan view
of advertising
in America—
what's wrong with it,
what's right with it,
how it works
and how it can be
made to work better*

The Trouble with Advertising . . .

John O'Toole

CHELSEA HOUSE

New York   London
1981

Printed and bound in the United States of America
Second printing January 1982

Library of Congress Cataloging in Publication Data

O'Toole, John
    The trouble with advertising.

    1. Advertising.   2. Advertising—United
States.   I. Title.
HF5821.086   659.1   81-38516
ISBN   0-87754-277-5   AACR2

Chelsea House Publishers
Harold Steinberg, Chairman & Publisher
Andrew E. Norman, President
Susan Lusk, Vice President
A Division of Chelsea House Educational Communications, Inc.
133 Christopher Street, New York 10014

For Phyllis, Sally and Ellen—in order of appearance

Contents

Introduction

"Funny," she said, "I can't believe you're in advertising."

She meant it as a compliment, I guess. For more than a year we'd been working together raising money for American Ballet Theatre. She apparently could not reconcile my interest in the arts, or perhaps my ability to read without moving my lips, with her obviously vivid stereotype of an advertising person.

Statistically speaking, it's very likely that this woman is one of the few people who actually know or have ever met an advertising person. In the United States there are only 50,000 of us working for firms that are members of the American Association of Advertising Agencies; perhaps 35,000 more work for the remaining agencies.

Of these, only a handful have anything to do with most of the magazine and network television advertising you see. About 40% of the total dollar volume of advertising placed through the 500 AAAA agencies is done by just ten of them. They employ only 17,000, many of whom live outside the United States. The remainder are concentrated mainly in New York, Chicago, Detroit, Los Angeles and San Francisco.

1

INTRODUCTION

So most Americans have never had the opportunity to learn, at a party, that the seemingly normal person they've just met makes his living at advertising—to pin him to the wall and launch a vigorous denunciation of the whole sordid business with that tedious preface "I'll tell you the trouble with advertising . . ."

As a practitioner of this much-maligned craft, I have always found such attitudes somewhat baffling. I once promised myself that if I woke up some morning, thought about what I do for a living and felt anything but elation about going to the office, I'd hang it up and go into free-lance writing. It's going on twenty-nine years now, and I'm still at it. That, in an age when "most men lead lives of quiet desperation," is something.

Of course, advertising is a highly demanding field. Since it is a service business and we can't forecast client emergencies, the hours are dreadful. It's hard on the constitution. It's hard on marriages. And success simply extends a sixty-hour work week to seventy hours, from which the IRS reaps a far richer harvest than you.

Advertising can be discouraging work, too. Sometimes what you consider your most glittering effort is trampled on by a callous client—or by your creative director. Sometimes, through no fault of yours, the agency loses an account and your job is in jeopardy. And the intellectuals and academicians, to say nothing of the general public, are fond of ridiculing advertising at every opportunity.

Why, then, would anyone want to dedicate the greater part of his waking hours to this bizarre craft? Well, it pays well. If you're good, it can pay very well. Because you're rewarded for results no matter what your age, race or gender, you can move ahead much faster than in most other businesses. And when you've got it going right, when the team is moving together like a *corps de ballet*, when you are transcending your own abilities and the competition lies stunned in your shining wake, you know it's worth the price. And you know you got a bargain.

More important, there are those of us who feel that the communications explosion is the central fact of the twentieth century, that we are involved in the most important aspect of contemporary society. For people burning with a compulsion to communicate ideas, facts, feelings and opinions—in print, on radio, over television, on film and on posters—there's no place else to be but advertising.

And while consumerists may not share our opinion, a lot of us feel that what we do is of vast, if often unappreciated, importance to our fellow citizens. There is no way for the American economic system to function without advertising. There is no other way to communicate enough information about enough products to enough people with enough speed.

It is probably apparent by now that I have a certain fondness for advertising. It is the fondness one feels for an old and thoroughly understood friend, and not, I assure you, an infatuation that blinds to reality.

I know some people scorn advertising because it is not as entertaining or challenging as the editorial or program material surrounding it. I know others assail it because it is so ubiquitous that to respond to it positively could be taken as enlisting in the proletariat. A birdwatcher cannot admit to an interest in sparrows. Since these conditions are part of its nature, I am fond of advertising because of them, not in spite of them.

I am fond of the people in advertising for similar reasons. I have worked among them for a long time, and most are bright, unconventional, irreverent, idealistic people who wouldn't be caught dead doing anything else. I know they are supposed to employ phrases like "Run it up the flagpole and see who salutes." I know they are often parodied by journalists, screenwriters and novelists because of the intensity with which they approach subjects that their critics consider boring or even banal. Since I regard their craft as neither, I admire and prize that intensity.

I'm telling you all this for two reasons: one, to alert you to the fact that while it values objectivity, the mind you are dealing with here is not untouched by bias when it comes to advertising; and two, to let you know how this book came about.

I was talking about advertising one day with Joy Johannessen, editor of Chelsea House Publishers. Like most in her calling,

INTRODUCTION

she displayed a point of view about my craft that, if not downright hostile, stopped several yards short of grudging acceptance. At some point in the warming dialogue, Joy made the preposterous suggestion that I write "a spirited defense of advertising."

Now, being of Irish descent, I feel an atavistic attraction to a good fight, the more hopeless the cause the better. In 1969, I infuriated most of the advertising community by advocating that television stop interrupting programs with commercials and begin "ganging" them together every half-hour—something similar to the European system. In 1970, I enraged the political community by decrying television spots on behalf of candidates for public office.

Those were quixotic adventures, but nothing to compare with the folly of "a spirited defense of advertising." I had seen the attitudes expressed about it in the polls. I had read the scathing books and articles. Better to be an advance man for the Ayatollah Khomeini or solicit contributions for Planned Parenthood in Vatican City. It was a naive and futile enterprise—which, of course, I immediately embraced.

The result, I hope, is less a spirited defense than an affirmation arrived at by means of a critical view from the inside. I will not try to convince you that advertising is without faults, nor will I expect you to love it. I will try to demonstrate that it is necessary, that it can be made better, and that in the process both the advertiser and the consumer will benefit. And I'll try to help you understand it.

Understanding it is the crucial first step to improving it, so that is the purpose of the first part of this book. The second describes the attitudes and approaches I believe must be brought to the practice of the craft in order to make advertising more effective, more efficient and more welcome. Part III gets into the way advertising is made, the steps in its development and the tools that are used. The purpose here is to point out how and when those proper attitudes and approaches should be applied along the way. Finally we'll get into various aspects and subspecies of advertising.

INTRODUCTION

If you emerge with a clearer understanding of what advertising is and does, you will have gained something. It has been estimated that you are exposed to some 1,600 advertising messages a day. If anything is following you around that doggedly, you're better off knowing what it's up to. If you put this book down feeling more kindly toward the whole business—and if you remember to tell that to the next pollster who quizzes you about your attitudes toward advertising—I will have gained something. And if you have a little fun along the way, we both will have gained something.

PART I

*Advertising—
a four-syllable
occupation
or a
four-letter
word?*

ATTITUDES ABOUT ADVERTISING

Advertising is an inescapable part of almost everyone's life in America. Thus, almost everyone has an attitude about the subject. And the attitudes, as expressed, seem extremely negative, in terms of both the product and those who produce it.

Back in 1975, Dr. Margaret Mead was quoted in one of our too-numerous trade journals as saying, "The only reason many people are in advertising is because no other business would pay them so much money." She added, "Most advertising people don't believe in the products they advertise or the words they are writing about their clients' products." In *The Lonely Crowd*, sociologist David Riesman writes, "Why, I ask, isn't it possible that advertising as a whole is a fantastic fraud, presenting an image of America taken seriously by no one, least of all by the advertising men who create it?"

According to a survey done in 1978 by Market Facts, Inc. for *Advertising Age* magazine, 43% of respondents not involved in advertising chose my craft as the one with "the lowest ethical standards." In 1977, a Gallup poll revealed the relative ranking of twenty occupational groups in terms of honesty and ethical standards. The public rated advertising practitioners nineteenth, just after labor union leaders and state officeholders. We did, however, beat car salesmen. The same year a Harris survey asked respondents how much confidence they had in the people who ran various institutions. Ad agencies ranked last. Humorist Kin Hubbard once characterized us this way: "It used to be that a fellow went on the police force when all else failed, but today he goes into the advertising game."

Now, I am no more insensitive to boors, scam artists, dolts and loudmouths than the next person. And over something more than a quarter of a century in advertising, though I've encountered a few of each, I've not noticed a disproportionate representation in my craft—certainly no more than among the lawyers, doctors, journalists, accountants, academicians, clergymen, clerks, civil servants and businessmen I've met.

Why do people feel that way about us? Was it something we said? Where do these staunchly held and mainly negative impressions come from? Well, a book entitled *The Hucksters* made a mighty contribution. It was published in 1946 by Frederick Wakeman, who, I'm grieved to admit, worked for the same agency I work for now (but so did Alan Jay Lerner, whose lyrics for *Camelot* provided a cheerier type of fantasy).

The Hucksters depicted ad people as fast-talking, double-dealing, hard-drinking scoundrels who yielded every ethical point to unscrupulous clients. It would probably have faded away on the remainder shelves had it not been made into a movie starring Clark Gable. The film was a hit and reappears to this day, like a spirit that cannot find eternal rest, on late-night television. Subsequent movies developed the stereotype into a character as morally impoverished as those in *The Hucksters* but far less acute. The adman became an exploitable hustler who was usually played by Jack Lemmon. With a few refinements, this persona surfaced as second banana in the television series *Bewitched*, in which Dick York added the further dimension of ineptitude.

Then, of course, self-destructive and self-serving advertising people contributed their share to what they perceived as an increasingly popular myth. Autobiographical books detailing the zany goings-on inside advertising agencies "where anything can happen and usually does" began to proliferate. Most bore the same relationship to advertising as *Dr. Doolittle* does to zoology, but the public loved them because they amused and didn't challenge the mind by questioning the stereotype. Foremost among these was *From Those Wonderful Folks Who Brought You Pearl Harbor* by Jerry della Femina. Jerry works hard at being an *enfant terrible* and masking the fact that he's a serious advertising practitioner. He succeeded at both in his book.

All of this has shaped the impressions people have of those of us in advertising. But it's not the whole story. There have been novels and TV programs and films aplenty about corrupt congressmen, venal businessmen and crooked lawyers, yet members of those occupations can attend cocktail parties relatively unassailed. The reason is that their activities affect most people indirectly or through third parties. At least the products of their efforts are less proximate, less numerous and less ubiquitous than is advertising.

Attitudes about advertising, which color attitudes about those who practice it, are obviously a concern to me. Because of the importance of advertising to a system that produces a lot of good living and good jobs for a lot of good people, it's worth looking into what those attitudes are, what has caused them, who is at fault and what can be done about it.

In the first instance, it's important to separate public attitudes—those measured by polling a sample of citizens representing all of us—from the attitudes of specialized publics: educators, journalists, consumer advocates and government. Each of the latter influence public opinion to some extent and should be looked at in terms of how and how much.

Whatever the influences, public attitudes toward advertising do not bring cheer to the heart of one who makes his living at it. A 1980 study by Yankelovich, Skelly & White reported that 70% of the American population was concerned with truth, distortion and exaggeration in advertising. A 1979 Louis Harris poll showed 81% feeling that "the claims for most products advertised on TV are exaggerated," and 52% saying that most or all TV advertising is "seriously misleading."

A survey conducted by my own company in 1977 found 36% of the national sample objecting to most TV advertising; the adjectives chosen most frequently were "dumb" and "juvenile." A 1974 study done by our industry association indicated that 59% of the respondents believed "most advertising insults the intelligence of the average consumer." It's interesting to note, however, that in the same study 88% said that advertising is essential, and 57% that advertising results in better products.

The professional critics come at us from a somewhat different direction. Since there are few more professional or critical than John Kenneth Galbraith, let us begin with him. In *The New Industrial State*, Galbraith says, "In everyday parlance, this great machine, and the demanding and varied talents that it employs, are said to be engaged in selling goods. In less ambiguous language, it means that it is engaged in the management of those who buy goods." Similarly, in his book *The Sponsor: Notes on a Modern Potentate*, Columbia University professor Erik Barnouw defines television advertising as "selling the unnecessary."

Philip Slater writes, in *The Pursuit of Loneliness*, "If we define pornography as any message from any communication medium that is intended to arouse sexual excitement, then it is clear that most advertisements are covertly pornographic." Novelist Mary McCarthy attacks us thusly in *On the Contrary*: "The thing, however, that repels us in these advertisements is their naive falsity to life. Who are these advertising men kidding? . . . Between the tired, sad, gentle faces of the subway riders and the grinning Holy Families of the Ad-Mass, there exists no possibility of even a wishful identification." I could go on and on were it not for a narrow threshold for self-inflicted pain. I'll conclude with a definition of advertising by Fred Allen: "85% confusion and 15% commission."

The criticisms leveled against advertising by the general public are clearly of a different nature than those of the specialized groups. The people are faulting advertising on what it's doing wrong or what it's not doing well enough or what it's doing too much of. The specialists are criticizing advertising on the basis of a totally different set of standards. The distinction is important because it explains why the advertising industry often responds so ineptly to its professional critics. It's hard to come up with answers when you not only don't understand the question but can't conceive why anyone would ask it.

The fact is that academicians, journalists, consumer advocates and government regulators criticize—and dislike—advertising because it isn't something else.

It accomplishes little to carry on about automobiles because they weren't made to fly or to reproach dogs because they don't climb trees. It is not in the nature of dogs to do what cats do, nor were the evolutionary forces that produced them guided by any imperative to develop that capacity. By the same token, it accomplishes little to condemn advertising because it isn't journalism or education or entertainment. It is fruitless to hold that advertising should be hidden, since it is not advertising if it's not seen. And it is witless to excoriate advertising for having arcane powers to brainwash or to make people act against their will when it clearly wouldn't and couldn't function as advertising if it did.

Yet such charges form the case made against advertising by many professional critics. Before I answer them, it's important for all of us to understand what advertising actually *is*. Only then can we put aside criticism based on what it isn't and get down to the positive challenge of making it better.

WHAT ADVERTISING IS

Archeologists have discovered evidence of some kind of advertising among the artifacts of every civilization that communicated by writing. The moment one man began growing or raising more than he needed and saw the opportunity to have what someone else was producing, the concept of bartering was born. Now, the only way to extend bartering beyond the chance encounter of two individuals with corresponding needs and surpluses was for each to post what he had and what he wanted in a public place where many could learn about it. The introduction of currency simplified the process by allowing people to post only what they were offering.

This "poster" concept dominated advertising for millennia. Its elements were the item or service offered, the name and location of the offerer, and sometimes the price. Often the most gifted artists of the era were employed to visualize for the prospect what he would receive for his money. Toulouse-Lautrec was one, and the graphics he created to lure customers into the Moulin Rouge now hang in the great art museums of the world.

Such embellishments brought a new dimension of creativity to the simple exposition of product, seller and price but did not change the basic approach; the poster remained the principal form of advertising until relatively recent years. As newspapers and magazines appeared, the poster concept was transferred to paid space in their pages. Early advertising agencies did little to advance the craft and develop its potential, for they had been formed essentially as brokers of space. They bought advertising space in quantity from newspapers and magazines at a 15% discount, then sold it to advertisers at full price. To justify this "commission," they counseled their clients on what to put in that space. But such advice was a relatively simple sideline to the space-brokering function since the poster concept more or less limited the information to product, seller and price.

In fact, in the early 1900s, the generally accepted definition of advertising was the one coined by the leading agency of the time (still in business today), N.W. Ayer. Ayer said advertising was "keeping your name before the public." But all that was to change with the new century. As a result of two men meeting in Chicago, the real energy of advertising was unlocked, its enormous potential tapped, and its true nature revealed.

One spring afternoon in 1904, in an office building at Wabash and Randolph Streets that was eventually replaced by Marshall Field's department store, two men were chatting. One was Ambrose Thomas, one of the founders of the Lord & Thomas advertising agency. The other was a bright young man named Albert Lasker, who, it was already apparent, would soon be running the agency. (More about both men and the agency later.)

Following a polite knock, an office boy came in with a note and handed it to Thomas. Upon reading it, Thomas snorted and gave it to Lasker. The note said: "I am downstairs in the saloon, and I can tell you what advertising is. I know that you don't know. It will mean much to me to have you know what it is and it will mean much to you. If you wish to know what advertising is, send the word 'yes' down by messenger." It was signed by a John E. Kennedy.

Thomas asked Lasker if he had ever heard of the man, and when Lasker said he hadn't, Thomas decided Kennedy was probably mad and wasn't worth wasting time on. But Lasker, who was dissatisfied with the concept of "keeping your name before the public," was willing to take a chance. He sent down for Kennedy, and the two spent an hour in Lasker's office. Then they headed for the saloon downstairs, not to emerge until midnight.

Kennedy was a former Royal Canadian Mounted Policeman, a dashing, mustachioed chap who in 1904 was employed as a copywriter for an elixir known as Dr. Shoop's Restorative.

JOHN O'TOOLE

What he said to Lasker that day resulted in his being hired on the spot for the unheard-of salary of $28,000 a year. Within twenty-four months, he was making $75,000.

What did he say to Lasker? Simply this: "Advertising is salesmanship in print."

It seems so simple and obvious today. But what this definition did in 1904 was to change the course of advertising completely and make possible the enormous role it now plays in our economy. For, by equating the function of an advertisement with the function of a salesman who calls on a prospect personally, it revealed the true nature of advertising.

For the first time, the concept of persuasion, which is the prime role of a salesman, was applied to the creation of advertising. Information was considered in a new light, since information is what a salesman must be equipped with and what he uses to persuade. An ad was seen as a means of conveying the personality of the advertiser, just as a good salesman reflects the standards of his company. Reason and logic became part of advertising planning. And so, for the first time, did the consumer.

With its possibilities revealed, advertising exploded. Now it could be refined, made more effective and applied to new tasks. Agencies proliferated, and those that understood the new definition flourished. None flourished more than Lord & Thomas, the birthplace of the revolution. Under Albert Lasker's leadership it became the biggest, most successful agency of its time.

WHAT ADVERTISING ISN'T

Advertising, then, is salesmanship functioning in the paid space and time of mass media. To criticize it for being that, for being true to its nature, is to question whether it should be permitted—a position taken by only the most rabid, none of whom have come up with a reasonable substitute for its role in the economy. And to criticize it for not being something else—something it might resemble but by definition can never be—is equally fruitless. Yet much of the professional criticism I spoke of has its feet planted solidly on those two pieces of shaky ground.

As a format for conveying information, advertising shares certain characteristics with journalism, education, entertainment and other modes of communication. But it cannot be judged by the same standards because it is essentially something else. This point is missed by many in government, both the regulators and the elected representatives who oversee the regulators.

The Federal Trade Commission was pushing not too long ago for one of those quasi-laws they call a Trade Regulation Ruling (when they were empowered to write the law of the land, I don't know; but that's another argument). This particular TRR would have required an ad or commercial for any product claiming to be nutritious to list all its nutritive elements. For two reasons advertising cannot comply with such a requirement and still end up as advertising.

One, advertising is salesmanship, and good salesmanship does not countenance boring the prospect into glassy-eyed semiconsciousness. Yet I am sure—and consumers on whom sample ads and commercials were tested agreed—that a lengthy litany of niacin, riboflavin, ascorbic acid and so on is as interesting as watching paint dry.

17

Less subjective is the fact that such a listing can't be given for many good, wholesome products within the confines of a thirty-second commercial. Since that's the standard length today, the end result of the proposed TRR would have been to ban those products from television advertising. The FTC staff did not consider that advertising necessarily functions in the paid space and time of mass media. Adding twenty or more seconds of Latin makes that impossible.

This example illustrates the problems that can arise when regulators try to dictate what must go into advertising. An FTC attorney named Donald F. Turner was quoted by Professor Raymond Bauer in a piece for the *Harvard Business Review* as saying, "There are three steps to informed choice. (1) The consumer must know the product exists. (2) The consumer must know how the product performs. (3) He must know how it performs compared to other products. If advertising only performs step one and appeals on other than a performance basis, informed choice cannot be made."

This is probably true in an ad for a new floor wax from S. C. Johnson or an antiperspirant from Bristol-Myers. But what about a new fragrance from Max Factor? How do you describe how Halston performs compared to other products? Is it important for anyone to know? Is it salesmanship to make the attempt? Or suppose you're advertising Coca-Cola. There can't be many people left in the world who don't know Coke exists or how it performs. Granted, there may be a few monks or aborigines who don't know how it performs in relation to other products, but you can't reach them through advertising. So why waste the time or space?

The reason Coca-Cola advertises is to maintain or increase a level of awareness about itself among people who know full well it exists and what it tastes like, people whom other beverage makers are contacting with similar messages about their products. Simple information about its existence and its popularity— information that triggers residual knowledge in the recipient about its taste and other characteristics—is legitimate and sufficient. It does what a salesman would do.

On the other hand, advertising for a big-ticket item—an automobile, for instance—would seemingly have to include a lot of information in order to achieve its end. But the advertising is not attempting to sell the car. It is an advance salesman trying to persuade the prospect to visit a showroom. Only there can the principal salesman do the complete job. Turner's definition is neither pertinent nor possible in the case of automobiles. In such cases mass communications media cannot convey the kind of information one needs in order to "know how the product performs" or to "know how it performs compared to other products." You have to see it, kick the tires, ask the salesman questions about it, let the kids try out the windshield wipers. And surely you have to drive it.

In the paid space and time of mass media, the purpose of automobile advertising is to select the prospect for a particular car and, on the basis of its appeal to his income, life-style or basic attitudes, to persuade him he's the person the designers and engineers had in mind when they created this model. If the information is properly chosen and skillfully presented, it will point out the relevance of the car to his needs and self-image sufficiently to get him into the showroom. Then it's up to the salesman to sell him the car—but with a different package of information, including the tactile and experiential, than could be provided in the ad.

From time to time some government regulator will suggest that advertising information should be limited to price and function. But consider how paleolithic that kind of thinking is. Restricting advertising to a discussion of price and function would eliminate, among other things, an equally essential piece of information: what kind of people make and market this product or provide this service.

The reputation, quality standards, taste and responsibility of the people who put out a product is information that's not only important to the consumer but is increasingly demanded by the consumer. It's information that can often outweigh price and function as these differences narrow among products within the same category. It's information that is critical to the advertising

19

my agency prepares for clients like Johnson's Wax, Sunkist Growers, Hallmark, Sears and many others. Advertising would not be salesmanship without it. Put it this way: if surgeons advertised and you had a hot appendix, would you want the ads to be limited to price and function information?

The government regulators, and the consumer advocates dedicated to influencing them, do not understand what advertising is and how it is perceived by the consumer. And their overwhelming fear that the one is always trying to deceive the other leads them to demand from advertising the kind of product information that characterizes *Consumer Reports*. They expect advertising to be journalism, and they evaluate it by journalistic standards. Since it is not, advertising, like the ugly duckling, is found wanting.

It is not in the nature of advertising to be journalistic, to present both sides, to include information that shows the product negatively in comparison with other entries in the category (unless, of course, the exclusion of such information would make the ad misleading or product usage hazardous). For example, advertising for Sunkist lemons, which might point out the flavor advantages of fresh lemons over bottled juice, should not be expected to remind people that fresh lemons can't be kept as long as a bottle of concentrate. Information is selected for journalism—or should be—to provide the recipient with as complete and objective an account as possible. Information is selected for advertising to persuade the recipient to go to a showroom or make a mental pledge to find the product on a store shelf.

Advertising, like the personal salesman, unabashedly presents products in their most favorable light. I doubt that there's a consumer around who doesn't understand that. For instance, would you, in a classified ad offering your house for sale, mention the toilet on the second floor that doesn't flush? I doubt that even a conscience as rigorous as Ralph Nader's would insist, in an ad to sell his own used car, on information about that worn fan belt or leaky gasket. No reader would expect it. Nor does anyone expect it from our clients.

Information, as far as advertising is concerned, is anything that helps a genuine prospect to perceive the applicability of a product to his or her individual life, to understand how the product will solve a problem, make life easier or better, or in some way provide a benefit. When the knowledge can't safely be assumed, it also explains how to get the product. In other words, it's salesmanship.

It is not witchcraft, another craft government regulators and otherwise responsible writers are forever confusing with mine. For the same reasons people like to believe that someone is poisoning our water supply or, as in the Joseph McCarthy era, that pinkos proliferate in our government and are trying to bring it down, someone is always rejuvenating the idea of subliminal advertising.

Subliminal advertising is defined as advertising that employs stimuli operating below the threshold of consciousness. It is supposed to influence the recipient's behavior without his being aware of any communication taking place. The most frequently cited example, never fully verified, involved a movie theater where the words "Drink Coke" were flashed on the screen so briefly that while the mind recorded the message, it was not conscious of receiving it. The result was said to be greatly increased sales of Coca-Cola at the vending counter.

I don't like to destroy cherished illusions, but I must state unequivocally that there is no such thing as subliminal advertising. I have never seen an example of it, nor have I ever heard it seriously discussed as a technique by advertising people. Salesmanship is persuasion involving rational and emotional tools that must be employed on a conscious level in order to effect a conscious decision in favor of one product over its competitive counterparts, and in order to have that decision remembered and acted upon at a later time. Furthermore, it's demeaning to assume that the human mind is so easily controlled that anyone can be made to act against his will or better judgment by peremptory commands he doesn't realize are present.

Even more absurd is the theory proposed by Wilson Bryan Key in a sleazy book entitled *Subliminal Seduction*. From whatever dark motivations, Key finds sexual symbolism in every ad

21

and commercial. He points it out to his readers with no little relish, explaining how, after reducing the prospect to a pliant mass of sexual arousal, advertising can get him to buy anything. There are some who might envy Mr. Key his ability to get turned on by a photograph of a Sunkist orange.

Most professional critics are much less bizarre in their condemnations. Uninformed about the real nature of advertising, perhaps, but not mad. For instance, they often ascribe recondite powers to advertising—powers that it does not have and that they cannot adequately define—because it is not solely verbal. Being for the most part lawyers and academics, they are uncomfortable with information conveyed by means other than words. They want things spelled out, even in television commercials, despite the fact that television is primarily a visual medium. They do not trust graphic and musical information because they aren't sure that the meaning they receive is the same one the consumer is receiving. And since they consider the consumer much more gullible and much less astute than they, they sound the alarm and then charge to the rescue. Sorcery is afoot.

Well, from time immemorial, graphics and music have been with us. I suspect each has been part of the salesman's tool kit for as long as there have been salesmen. The songs of medieval street vendors and Toulouse-Lautrec's Jane Avril attest.

A mouth-watering cake presented photographically as the end benefit of Betty Crocker Cake Mix is just as legitimate as and more effective than a verbal description. The mysteriously exuberant musical communication "I Love New York" honestly conveys the variety of experiences offered by New York State; it is not witchcraft. It is not to be feared unless you fear yourself. But perhaps that is the cradle that spawns consumer advocates and government regulators. There is something murky in that psyche, some kink in the mentality of those who feel others are incapable of making mundane decisions for themselves, something Kafka-like in the need to take over the personal lives of Americans in order to protect them from themselves.

I read with growing disquiet a document put out by the staff of the Federal Trade Commission in 1979 entitled *Consumer*

Information Remedies. In discussing how to evaluate consumer information, they wrote,

> The Task Force members struggled long and hard to come up with a universally satisfactory definition of the *value* of consumer information. Should the Commission consider a mandatory disclosure to be a valuable piece of information, for instance, if it were later shown that although consumers understood the information, they did not use it when making purchase decisions? Is there a value in improving the *quality* of market decisions through the provision of relevant information, or is it necessary for the information to change behavior to have value?

The ensuing "remedies" make it clear that the staff really judges the value of a mandatory disclaimer by the degree to which it changes consumer behavior in the direction they are seeking.

But wait a minute. I'm a consumer, too. Who are they to be wondering what to do with me next if I understand but choose to ignore some dumb disclaimer they've forced an advertiser to put in his ad? It's my God-given right to ignore any information any salesman presents me with—and an ad, remember, is a salesman. And what's this about changing behavior? Well, mine is going to change if the employees of a government I'm paying for start talking like that out loud. It's going to get violent.

Later in the same document, the staff addresses "Sub-Optional Purchases." While I have no quarrel with their intent, I find my hackles rising as they define the problem in terms of people "misallocating resources," consumers wasting their dollars on "products that do not best satisfy their needs." Listen, fellows, those are *my* resources you're talking about. Those are *my* dollars, what there is of them after you guys in Washington have had your way with my paycheck. I'm going to allocate them as I damn well please. And if I want to waste a few on products that do not best satisfy my needs—an unnutritious but thoroughly delicious hotdog at the ball park, for example—try to stop me.

Perhaps I, in turn, am seeking evidence of conspiracy. Perhaps I'm looking under beds. But I think I understand the true nature of government bureaucrats. They, on the other hand, do not understand that of advertising. They and other professional critics—the journalists, consumerists, academicians—don't understand that it's not journalism or education and cannot be judged on the basis of objectivity and exhaustive, in-depth treatment. Thorough knowledge of a subject cannot be derived from an advertisement but only from a synthesis of all relevant sources: the advertising of competitors, the opinions of others, the more impartial reports in newspapers, magazines and, increasingly, television.

The critics also don't understand that advertising isn't witchcraft, that it cannot wash the brain or coerce someone to buy what he doesn't want. It shouldn't be castigated for what it cannot and does not purport to do. And it isn't entertainment, either. A commercial should offer some reward to the viewer in return for his time, but that reward need not always take the form of entertainment. Sometimes the tone should be serious, even about seemingly frivolous subjects. Hemorrhoids are not funny to those who have them.

Advertising sometimes resembles other fields, just as an elephant resembles a snake to the blind man who feels its trunk, and a tree to another who feels its leg. But advertising is really salesmanship functioning in the paid space and time of mass media. As we shall see, we can find enough reasons to criticize advertising without flailing it for not being what it isn't.

THE IMPLICIT CONTRACT

Pointing out to the professional critics that their arguments are generally based on a misunderstanding of advertising seldom discourages further attacks. For fundamentally their quarrel is less with advertising than with the concept of free choice that underlies a free marketplace, the essential environment of advertising.

The critics regard it as wasteful to have seven brands of bar soap competing for the consumer's favor with large advertising expenditures. I regard it as an opportunity, rare in the world today, for the consumer to learn about and choose exactly the features, color, fragrance and shape he'd like. They see it as frivolous to introduce product features or conveniences that to them seem minor and add to the cost. I see it as offering a choice to those who consider the feature or convenience worth the price. They view as irresponsible the advertising of a product that under certain conditions of use or misuse or excessive use could possibly be dangerous to someone. As long as those conditions are sufficiently well known, I view it as part of the freedom to choose, to assume risk, to lead a free life.

For these critics, the trouble with advertising is the trouble they perceive with the free marketplace and our whole economic system. In this much larger debate, I have heard their arguments and remain unconvinced, along with the vast majority of Americans.

Of far more concern to me are the negative attitudes about advertising expressed by the general public. These are consumers whose goodwill is important to me and whose response to the advertising we do for our clients is essential to the continuation of my mortgage payments. I respect their judgment and fear their wrath—sentiments I don't detect in the professional critics, who are forever trying to protect the hapless consumer from his own gullibility, poor judgment and blind stupidity. To read a Federal Trade Commission document is to envision the American citizen as Candide, bumbling innocently through the grasping hands of charlatans, seeking a Pangloss.

I know a different consumer. I have watched him operate in the marketplace for decades now, driving inferior products off the shelves in a month by his refusal to repurchase, halting the sales of a product with no unique features when its price rose a few pennies above that of competitors, forcing manufacturers to eat inventories and retool when the feature he wanted in a product wasn't available. American consumers are the canniest of creatures. I speak as one whose not infrequent mistakes have been immediately made manifest by them. And they are powerful, despite the professional critics' insistence that they are helpless pawns of advertising.

The mightiest weapon consumers have, and the one manufacturers fear most, is their refusal to repurchase. Advertising is powerful in that it can get them to buy a product once. But if it doesn't please them, the heaviest media budget in the world won't get them to buy it again. And if enough of them respond that way, the manufacturer has lost his investment in research, development, production, sales, advertising—everything. Big dollars. In addition, his sales force is demoralized, his credibility with the trade is tarnished, and people in his marketing department and at his advertising agency are looking for other jobs.

When you consider that this fate awaited 66% of the new products introduced in 1979, you gain respect for consumers' critical faculties and their power. And if you make your living in advertising, you have to be concerned about the opinions expressed by these formidable folks whose wrath is so fearful.

I can discount some of those opinions on the basis that the general is usually trusted less than the specific. Salesmen, as a class, have always been regarded with some suspicion. Their goal, after all, is to separate you from your money. But a particular salesman, the one who sells you those neckties your wife always likes—he's all right. Especially if he provides you with personalized service, such as making sure they go with your suits and shirts. Especially if he's a nice guy. I've never met anyone who thought highly of life insurance salesmen as a group. Ah, but *my* agent is another matter. He's different.

People I meet at parties, once they discover how I make my living, feel compelled to tell me about the low regard in which they hold advertising. But in return for my listening to their complaints, they have to answer some questions too. I ask them what they think of Hallmark's advertising, or Kraft's, or the Raid advertising with those cute bugs. Oh, well, that's different.

People who hate advertising often love ads. It's interesting to note that in the 1979 Louis Harris study cited earlier, the one in which 52% of the people said most or all TV advertising is misleading, 59% cited specific examples of TV advertising they liked. Only 32% said that none of it appealed to them.

Another thing those frequenters of cocktail parties are fond of telling me is that they are unusual, that they pay no attention to advertising and aren't influenced by it at all. One woman made this claim while smoking a Kent III. At the time, Kent III was such a new product that she couldn't have heard of it any other way than through advertising.

It is a matter of pride, I suppose, to contend that advertising only has an effect on the purchasing decisions of those who attended an inferior university or, heaven help us, none at all. But I have seen the requests for a recipe come into the Kraft Kitchens as a result of an offer buried in the copy. I've looked at the zip codes, and I know who's cutting those coupons out of our Literary Guild ads and sending them in with a check. I know, too, who's sending in for brochures about Bermuda, addressing their requests to the postal box number that appeared only in our ad. It is you, standing on my neighbor's patio with a white wine spritzer in one hand and my lapel in the other as you tell me you pay no attention to advertising. If it makes you feel better, fine.

Advertising expenditures have grown at a faster rate than the economy in recent years. This growth was minimally affected by the 1980 recession. American businesses spent over $55 billion on advertising in 1980, more than is spent annually by the entire American public on jewelry, watches, shoes, furniture and bedding combined. Companies are not spending this money because they want to provide the people in their advertising agencies with a more comfortable life. They are investing in advertising because advertising returns the investment manyfold. Advertising does that because people respond to it by buying products. All kinds of people. Even those who deny it vigorously.

The real question is, if people respond to it to such an extent, why do they express such dislike for it? Is it simply a case of disdain for the general overriding regard for the specific, as with life insurance salesmen? Is it some form of neo-snobbism? Is it important? It's all of the above, but it's a good deal more. It has to do with broken contracts.

I believe that a contract, or at least an understanding, exists between the American public and the American advertiser concerning what advertising is, what its limitations are and what price the people will pay for it. This contract is unwritten, unspoken and perhaps unconscious. It is beyond or beneath the comprehension of the professional critics, but it is so clearly accepted by consumers that they can respond to some of the efforts of government regulators with nothing but laughter.

The contract, were it ever to be written, would read something like this:

> I'm an advertiser. You're a consumer. I'm going to communicate to you through advertising. Now, advertising, as we both know, is salesmanship functioning in the paid space and time of mass communications media. That's all it is. Like any salesman, its purpose is commercial. It's going to present products and services in their best light. It's not going to tell you what's good about the other guy's product or service. There are plenty of ways for you to find out about that (see my competitor's contract under separate cover). It's going to be corny at times; maybe there'll

be a little too much of it now and then. We're all
human.

But I promise you this. My advertising won't lie to
you, and it will not deliberately try to mislead you.
It won't bore the hell out of you or treat you as
though you were a fool or embarrass you or your
family. But remember, it's a salesman. Its purpose is
to persuade you to trade your hard-earned cash for
my product or service.

In return for your putting up with all this, I'm
going to support those newspapers and magazines
and radio stations and TV programs you like so
much. I'm going to pay for music, situation comedies, news, stories, movies, variety shows, football
games, cartoon shows and reportage on every aspect
of life you may be interested in.

In the process you'll get a lot of important information to help you make informed choices. And
you'll get what those lawyers call "puffery." You'll
get news about new products you'll like, and you'll
be persuaded to try some you'll never buy again.
That's the way it goes.

What do you say? Is it a deal? Great. I'm glad we
understand each other.

That's the implicit contract, and I believe it's fully understood
by every adult and child in America, because each of us has
grown up surrounded by advertising, responding to it and enjoying its benefits. Some who refuse to sign the contract become
consumer advocates or join the meager ranks of their official
constituency. Others become government regulators or anti-
advertising journalists. Academicians have to renounce the contract upon arrival on campus or they won't be allowed into the
faculty lounge. But the dropouts are few. The vast majority
have agreed to go along. Thus, when the implicit contract is
broken, people get mad. Understandably so.

It is not advertising itself but its violation of the contract that has resulted in negative attitudes on the part of those who really matter—consumers. The violations have taken one of three forms, each of which is clearly prohibited by the contract, and each of which would be unacceptable behavior on the part of a personal salesman. There have been cases of false or deliberately misleading statements. There have been cases where, contrary to the wording of the first clause, the purpose has not been commercial but something far more grave and far-reaching. And there have been cases of criminal boredom or unaggravated assault on the intelligence.

We'll discuss each of these forms a bit because the implications are important to an understanding of how public attitudes have been affected and whether or not they can be improved.

False and Misleading Ads

Since a good salesman never lies about his product, an ad breaks the contract with the consumer when it makes false or misleading claims. "False" and "misleading" describe two different offenses, either of which can occur inadvertently. Strict interpretation might call an ad false if it promises that the product is "at your grocer's now" and your particular grocer happens to be out of stock. Some authorities contend that an advertisement is misleading if there is evidence that consumers misunderstand part of it. But a fascinating study completed in 1980 by Professor Jacob Jacoby of Purdue University—a study that gave us our first real insight into how people receive televised information—belies that claim.

The study subjected 2,700 people across the country to thirty-second pieces of television communication. There were three kinds of communication represented: commercials, noncommercial messages for causes such as the United Negro College Fund, and normal programming. The latter included news, situation comedies, and adventure and mystery shows such as *Charlie's Angels* and *Barnaby Jones*. After the viewing, the participants

30

were asked six questions to determine whether or not they understood what they saw and heard.

In 83% of the cases people misunderstood at least part of what they saw. The degree of miscomprehension went from 50% to 11%. Professor Jacoby concluded that viewers will normally misunderstand between one-fourth and one-third of what they see on television. As a sidelight, the study noted that commercials are less likely to be miscomprehended than program material. The difference is small but statistically significant.

But this kind of discussion, while it demonstrates that eliminating false and misleading advertising is not as easy as it appears, doesn't resolve the issue. For our purposes, a false ad is one that deliberately puts forth untrue information about the product. A deceptive ad is one that deliberately gives an impression about the product that cannot be supported in fact. Or, in either case, an ad that is so *perceived* by a substantial portion of the audience to whom it was directed, even if the intent was not there.

This is the most serious breach of the implicit contract that can occur, for it leaves a group of consumers suspicious of the process. If they experience another breach, they become cynical. Enough violations observed by enough people will lead them to conclude that the contract is worthless, and then advertising will no longer work. The fact that it does work, and works so well, is evidence that most people have not drawn that conclusion. But every false or misleading ad that appears is, to those of us who value the living we make at this craft, a personal attack. It must be prevented from happening. Or, if it has happened, it must be exposed, stopped, and the perpetrators discouraged from repeating the offense.

I wish I could claim total victory in the war on the false and misleading, but more of it goes on than you or I would like, particularly at the local level. There are still used car dealers misrepresenting their cars or prices in commercials. There are still retailers doing "bait and switch" cons in which they lure you in with an ad for a highly desirable bargain solely to sell you something else at a higher price. All of this is illegal but difficult to police. The Council of Better Business Bureaus keeps after it in most areas. But even after their best efforts have resulted in the advertiser being punished, some consumer has been burned and his faith in the contract shaken if not shattered.

Not all offenses are at the grass-roots level. In many national magazines there is still a highly questionable neighborhood that they refer to as "back-of-the-book," a small-space ghetto for mail order ads. Some are perfectly legitimate, but there are far too many promises made there for magic bust developing creams, hair restorers, quick correspondence courses to make you an overnight literary lion, and books on how to become a millionaire in thirty days. Magazines, whose future depends as much on the implicit contract as mine does, have to grow up and turn down that kind of trash.

But for the most part, national advertising is far freer of false and misleading advertising than the public wants to believe. Certainly there now exist abundant safeguards to prevent it from appearing, or from continuing should it slip through. For example, magazines and newspapers, particularly the larger ones, check every advertisement submitted to them for accuracy of claim. Granted, the resources available to them for verification are limited, but they try. Some, like *Good Housekeeping*, actually subject products to laboratory testing.

A television commercial submitted to a station belonging to the National Association of Broadcasters—and most stations do belong—must abide by the NAB Code. Any commercial directed to children, any for personal products, any for foods, vegetable oils or margarines that mentions fat or cholesterol, must be thoroughly checked by the Code Review Board. And they are rigorous—sometimes, in the opinion of some of us, ludicrously so. I know of one commercial, done for a doll manufacturer, that contained a reference to the "skin" of the doll. The Code Review Board rejected it on the basis that the covering was not actually skin but a variety of plastic. For some reason the advertiser was allowed to refer to that stuff on the doll's head as "hair."

What the Code Review Board does for stations, the Standards

and Practices Department does for the three networks. Every commercial submitted for a network spot must be cleared by these humorless but thorough censors. Since their meticulous rummaging through the proposed words and pictures of a thirty-second commercial goes into areas of taste and propriety as well as truth and accuracy, you can imagine the friction that results between creator and critic. In the long run the arguments are little more than an amusing by-product of a system necessary to prevent damaging breaches of the contract.

In addition there are numerous checks of proposed copy by battalions of lawyers on the advertiser side and on the agency side, for both are held equally responsible under the law for false or misleading claims. But should one slip through, the final official court for meting out punishment is the Consumer Protection Division of the Federal Trade Commission. The FTC can impose fines and other penalties, including forcing the advertiser to run "corrective" advertising to undo the damage done by his previous claims.

While this sword is terrible, it is anything but swift. Formal FTC proceedings may take several years. At least one has gone on for twenty. By the time the matter is settled, the aggrieved consumer has lost faith not only in advertising but in his government. And he's paid dearly, as a taxpayer, in the process. Government is unsurpassed in its ability to turn the simple into the complex—and costly.

It was this situation, plus a recognition of the harm false and misleading advertising can do to the system that supports us, that in 1971 led the advertising industry to establish its own self-regulatory body, the National Advertising Review Board. The purpose was to provide a further level of deterrence between the clearance of advertising copy by the publication or the broadcaster and the punitive but inefficient response of government.

The National Advertising Review Board is sponsored by advertisers, media, agencies and the Council of Better Business Bureaus. The latter has set up a National Advertising Division, which receives complaints about false and misleading advertising from consumers and consumerists, from competitive advertisers and from its own staff, which monitors ads in all media. The staff takes complaints directly to the advertisers and, most frequently, resolves the issue there. But if the advertiser is unable to substantiate the claim in question and refuses to change or cancel the advertising, the issue goes to the NARB.

The Board comprises thirty representatives from companies that advertise nationally, ten from advertising agencies and ten "public" members—what I have been referring to as professional critics. When a complaint comes to the NARB, the chairman appoints a five-person panel: three from advertising companies, one from an agency and one public member. The panel determines whether the claim is substantiated and the case should be closed or the advertising is false or misleading and should be stopped. In the latter case, should the advertiser refuse to comply, all the records are turned over to the FTC, with attendant publicity, and all hell breaks loose.

In its first nine years the NARB has not had to take this extreme action in a single case. Of the 1,739 complaints handled by the National Advertising Division, 703 of the ads were voluntarily modified or discontinued by the advertiser, 661 were judged to contain legitimate and substantiated claims, and 315 were administratively closed because they did not involve matters of truth and accuracy. Of the 35 cases referred to an NARB panel, the judgment went in favor of the advertiser in 14 of them, against in 21. At the time of this writing, 46 cases were in the works at the NAD. Though it may take several months for a complaint to make its way through the NARB machinery, it's a big improvement on the pace of government.

We might hope for a greater volume of cases, but all in all the NARB has done a fine job in its first decade. Since my opinion may be colored by my active involvement from the beginning, let me quote none other than the former chairman of the Federal Trade Commission, Michael Pertschuk.

> Day in and day out at the FTC we plug away in
> pursuit of the ideal marketplace: entrepreneurial, in-

novative, unfettered and, above all, competitive. But
we also have competitors, and in one marketplace
we're taking a beating: the competition to clean up
shoddy and deceptive advertising. The NARB has
shamelessly cornered the market. You've skinned the
cream of deceptive ads, outrageous frauds and mis-
representations. Thanks to you, the latter-day ances-
tor of the silver-tongued snake oil purveyor has been
tongue-tied. At least in the national media.

Another commissioner not celebrated for handing out bouquets
to advertising folks, Robert Pitofsky, said, "After about seven or
eight years of vigorous operation, I think we have enough evidence to conclude that the NARB is as successful an effort at
self-regulation as any we've seen in this country."

Perhaps. But more is needed. The sphere of the NARB has to
be expanded. Local advertising has to be policed better. Only
when all such breaches of the contract are eliminated will I rest
easier about the future of the young people we're bringing into
advertising today. Only then will I be safe from the assailants at
cocktail parties and their disquisitions on "the trouble with
advertising . . ." And only then can I make the long-awaited
suggestion that there's no further need for the Consumer Protection
Division of the FTC.

Impersonations of Ads

A good salesman does not misrepresent his purpose. If your
insurance agent calls and says he'd like to drop by because he
has something important to tell you, if he arrives in his usual
polyester suit and blow-dried hair with bulging briefcase in
hand, if he sits down in your living room and suddenly begins
attempting to convert you to Zoroastrianism, you have legitimate cause to feel he's broken an implicit contract with you.

Similarly, when you are approached under circumstances that

35

would lead anyone to expect, given the conditions of the implicit contract, that someone is going to try to sell you a soft drink, an aspirin or a chain saw, and you gradually perceive that his purpose is to get you to help make him president of the United States, you have reason to feel that the contract has been broken, that you've been had and something is very wrong somewhere.

A magazine or newspaper ad for a political candidate represents a less serious breach than a TV commercial since the reader can quickly ascertain what the purpose is, who's behind it and whether or not to pursue the matter further. The same is true of a poster (in addition to which, it's been used for political purposes almost as long as for commercial ones). But to employ the formats, techniques and trappings of the television spot to lure viewers into a shallow substitute for a candidate's presentation of his qualifications is a subtle form of deception demeaning to both the political process and advertising.

I have debated this issue for a decade, on platforms, in print and on *The Today Show*, with the "media specialists" hired by aspirants to public office. They continue to demand, "What's the difference between selling a candidate and selling a product?" If they don't know—or, more important, if the candidates who hire them don't know—then God help the Republic.

A product represents a relatively minor expenditure. If the advertising misleads, consumers have the most powerful retaliatory weapon of all at their disposal: refusal to repurchase. If it is one of those big-ticket items I mentioned, one for which the advertising is simply trying to get them into a showroom or dealership to feel and experience the product, they'll probably receive some sort of warranty when they buy. If the product doesn't work, they can take it back. If the manufacturer won't fix it or reimburse them, they can sue. What recourse do they have after "buying" a candidate on the basis of promises made in a TV spot and unfulfilled in office?

The purpose of product advertising is to increase share of market. Every category—detergents, canned soup, paper towels—has a number of products vying within it. Each has, at any given time, a certain percentage of the total dollar sales in the category. Each is advertising in order to increase his percentage at the expense of the other guy. It's a thoroughly normal and, to the consumer, beneficial process. It's also a continuing process. Each contender knows there are things he could do that would boost sales today but lose more tomorrow. Things like making promises he can't keep. Or lying about the competitor. Or creating an impression with imagery that has no bearing on reality.

Political advertising, while deceptively similar to product advertising on the surface, is dictated by a totally different set of rules. And that is why it violates the contract from the outset. There are no market shares involved in political advertising. Whereas product advertising is based on the continual "elections" that take place every hour of the day, every day of every week, in stores all over America, political advertising is rooted in the reality of a single election in which one "product" wins 100% of the market and the other is put out of business. And the stakes are so high that toward the end of the campaign the temptation to lie and mislead is overwhelming. Why not? If you win, who can take it away from you? If you lose, what does it matter?

During the 1972 campaign I was asked to be part of an advisory council to the November Group, the advertising agency formed to promote Richard Nixon's election. Because of the positions I had taken on political advertising, and because friends urged me to put those views into practice, I agreed. The leader of the agency was Pete Dailey, an old friend and an advertising practitioner I admired. Later Pete headed the agency that worked, in 1980, on behalf of Ronald Reagan, and I joined him in a similar capacity on that campaign.

The commercials the group produced for Nixon's campaign were in my view excellent, primarily because they didn't masquerade as "spots." They were documentary films in five-minute and one-minute lengths. They dealt with substantive issues and supported them with actual accomplishments. But they never ran. Other forces in the White House—led, I was told, by Bob

Haldeman (an advertising man *manqué*)—had another group producing thirty-second spots that never showed Nixon, or anyone else, on camera. They talked about how vacillating McGovern was, while showing a weathervane with George's face flipping back and forth with the wind. They talked about how dangerous his defense policy was while showing a hand disdainfully sweeping warships off a chessboard. They said nothing.

If my agency had tried to advertise a product that way, the networks would have turned the copy down, the NAB Code Review Board would have turned it down, our lawyers would have turned it down. If none of those things had happened and the commercials had actually run, the competitor would have brought the case before the NARB. But none of these safeguards pertain with political advertising, which is another reason it represents a violation of the contract.

I left the Nixon campaign sadder but wiser. I at least knew something about the candidate who would sanction such a thing and the men surrounding him who would initiate it. The average voter, unfortunately, didn't find out until Richard Nixon left the White House in disgrace. (My experience with the Reagan campaign, by the way, was a good deal more reassuring.)

But Nixon was not alone. Dwight Eisenhower and John F. Kennedy ran singing commercials with cartoon visuals that said absolutely nothing of substance. James Buckley, campaigning for the Senate in New York in 1970, ran a commercial in which he never appeared. It featured John Wayne talking about what a good fellow Buckley was. It goes on and on to this day and to our shame. What can be done about it? We have to separate the televised political message from the formats, conventions and techniques with which people have come to associate—and by which they recognize—a commercial for something of far less significance.

We might learn a lesson from our British cousins. Under their Television Act, political commercials are forbidden. However, during general elections the two network organizations—BBC and ITV—allocate a certain number of free broadcasts to each party, the number based generally on the membership of the party.

After a year-long study headed by Newton Minow, the Twentieth Century Fund recommended something similar for the United States—one of the few nations in the world, incidentally, that allow political candidates to purchase TV time. The Fund suggested that during the last five weeks of a presidential campaign, all TV and radio stations simultaneously carry six prime-time half-hour programs featuring the candidates and attempting to "illuminate campaign issues and give the audience insight into the abilities and personal qualities of the candidates."

The Fund's recommendations point to the importance of the *kind* of political message to be used. Ten-second, thirty-second, even sixty-second lengths are inadequate and inappropriate for presenting a candidate to the voter. These lengths defy a discussion of issues and encourage the shallowest kind of imagery, the shoddiest kind of logic and the most reprehensible mudslinging. They should remain the province of product advertising. If the broadcasting industry were to set a five-minute minimum on political messages, many of the abuses would automatically be eliminated. Since candidates can purchase such time segments at the rate charged for program material rather than at commercial rates, the cost for five minutes is far less than for a thirty-second spot.

Barring such sweeping changes, at an absolute minimum candidates should be held personally responsible for all messages placed on their behalf, just as any other advertiser is. They should not be allowed to disclaim messages placed by "Citizens for Jones" or whatever the shadow committee may be called. In addition, a few guidelines could easily be imposed without unduly restricting the creative construction of the message. Here are three that I believe should be a code for political broadcast messages, a code that candidates themselves would have to assent to in writing before they or their supporters could be sold time on any station.

1. The message should be designed to help the voter know and understand the candidate, his character and his ability to communicate.

2. The message should establish the issues the
candidate feels are important.

3. The message should clearly state where the candidate stands on these issues.

These changes would go a long way towards forcing political
advertising into formats that would not confuse it with product
advertising. But until the "media specialists" and the advertising
agencies that handle this kind of communication cease equating
a candidate and an office with a deodorant and an armpit,
intelligent citizens will continue to feel they've been taken, that
the contract has been broken. And we will all be poorer for it.

Boring and Insulting Ads

Does anyone really sit down at the typewriter resolved to write
a dull ad or commercial, or one that will insult the intelligence
of the reader or viewer?

There are a few benighted advertisers and advertising agency
people who truly believe they are addressing a mass audience
with, as the myth has it, a twelve-year-old's mentality. We will
deal with them later. There are others who, themselves, have a
twelve-year-old's mentality, who truly believe that the banal
little messages they manufacture are of interest to someone, and
who are insensitive enough to be able to ignore sensitivity in
others. Time and the marketplace will deal with them.

But I have found these types to be rare, at least in national
advertising. More often dullness results from a well-intended
but slavish reliance on "objective" influences. Copy testing is
one of these influences and is responsible for far more dull
advertising than are dull advertising people.

Copy testing is an attempt to simulate in a laboratory the
effect of a message delivered by mass communication. Most
frequently it is perpetrated on television commercials, usually in
a form short of the finished film—drawings, for example, put on

"slide film" accompanied by a sound track. These "animatics" are shown to groups of people in a theater or small room, and the respondents are asked questions about them. Their answers are numerically processed, and "scores" of various kinds are assigned to the proposed commercial.

Clearly the copy testing environment differs from the environment in which people normally view a television commercial. Hence, their answers to questions will differ from what their undirected responses would be at home. They are watching under forced conditions and are being asked to play expert.

And the fault lies not only in the contrived viewing situation of the respondents but in the eyes of their beholders. As copy testing scores accumulate over the years, advertising people tend to sift through them seeking similarities among high-scoring commercials in various product categories. They then—and here is the fatal flaw in logic—try to impose upon future commercials those perceived similarities in high-scoring past commercials. Since originality of thought, vividness of language and genius in casting are difficult for the statisticians to identify from one commercial to another, more obvious commonalities are sought. Was it a little drama or one person talking directly to us? If it was a drama, did it take place in a home or a public place? If it was one person, was the score higher if that person happened to be a celebrity? How many seconds elapsed before the product was mentioned?

Questions like these probably have as little to do with high scores as the answers of copy test interviewees have to do with the real responses of people in their living rooms. Nevertheless the questions are asked, and the answers carefully studied. And thus—since we are all more at ease mulling over the past than divining the future—are formats born. If two women talking in a kitchen drew a high score last time, obviously two women of the same type talking in the same kitchen will work the next time. Indeed, two women talking in a kitchen will be dictated as the format for the next commercial, despite the fact that the product is different, despite the fact that the prospect is different.

Interesting, involving advertising is built on ideas. A format is not an idea, no matter how much the behavioristic school of advertising would like it to be. Thus format commercials are, to many of us, dull.

You might be thinking now that the programs during which they appear are at least as dull. While seemingly irrelevant to the point I'm trying to make, that is both interesting and true—a combination seldom achieved. Most prime-time half-hour or one-hour programs are dull as dust. Could it be because most are created according to formats dictated by statisticians who have studied the Nielsen numbers to determine what worked and didn't work last season? Could the same magic formula be responsible for the cornucopia of boredom, in both commercials and programming, that is our television screen during prime-time network hours?

Formats explain part of the dullness the public ascribes to advertising, but certainly not all. And they don't explain the other refrain we hear so frequently—advertising's capacity to "insult my intelligence." There must be a more fundamental reason for this complaint, which is a consistent response to surveys and a clearly articulated warning from consumers that the implicit contract is being dangerously strained if not patently violated. And there is: the nature of television.

You may have noticed that in discussing dull or "insulting" advertising, I've leaned toward "commercial" rather than "ad." The noun "commercial" generally denotes a television advertisement, and this is the provocation for almost all public outcry about dullness or insults to the intelligence. The previously mentioned back-of-the-book ads in some magazines are cited as being offensive, but not often. Television commercials are the problem. They are, on these two counts at least, the primary violators of the contract. And the principal reasons for this lie in the nature of the medium itself and the way in which it has developed in the United States.

It is the nature of television to be linear or sequential. The same is true of radio. It flows out at us in a continuous stream from the moment we turn it on until the moment we turn it off. One thing ends and another begins without our control; all we can do is ignore it. And ignoring it, especially the compelling combination of picture and sound represented by television, is difficult for most.

Print media are particular. Each page is a particle that is evaluated in turn and in an instant. In that instant you make a decision as to whether you'll spend time with it or not, and you make similar judgments about each element on that page. The decision is yours.

Thus, when an ad is boring or represents an insult to your intelligence, you evaluate and pass over it in less than a second. Unless it is extremely offensive, you'll probably never remember seeing it. A commercial, on the other hand, is there—right there with you in your living room—whether or not you've decided it's dull or dumb. And it's there until it chooses to end or you choose to switch channels. But by that time you're probably muttering that advertising is boring or that it insults your intelligence.

It is in the nature of television, too, to be intrusive. This is due partially to its alluring mélange of graphics, motion, color, voices and music. It is also due to its novelty and to the disproportionate attention paid it in this, its adolescence if not infancy. We pick up a newspaper at specific and habitual moments of leisure. We pick up a magazine when the mood strikes us. We turn on our television set when we enter the room, like a lamp. Children seem to require it as part of the environment, like air. Lonely people use it for companionship. The average household in our country has it on five and a half hours a day. At that rate, even if only a small minority of commercials were dull or insulting to the intelligence, it would be difficult to avoid them.

The manner in which television developed in the United States exacerbated these conditions. To understand how, let us digress for a moment into a mini-history of commercial television. The story begins with, and is inseparable from, the development of commercial radio.

The first radio station, KDKA, Pittsburgh, owned by Westinghouse, commenced broadcasting in November 1920. Within two years some four hundred more stations were licensed. Commercial radio actually began when AT&T instituted what it called "toll broadcasting" on its New York station, WEAF. For a fee, anyone might enter the station as he would a phone booth and address the public as he would a friend. An enterprising advertising man, William H. Rankin, was one of the first to buy time and test the concept. His success resulted in the signing of sixteen sponsors within six months.

No sales message as such was involved in these sponsored broadcasts. Gillette would provide a talk on fashions in beards, or a toothpaste manufacturer one on dental care. The first weekly one-hour series, sponsored by the Browning King clothing firm, provided a new format: entertainment with sponsor identification limited to the name of the entertainers. Thus we had the Browning King Orchestra, the Gold Dust Twins, the Ipana Troubadours and others.

This method of "indirect advertising" was still in general use when the first radio network, NBC, was founded in 1926. But the economic pressures of the Depression and the competitive pressure of another network, CBS, gradually resulted in a change of approach. By the early 1930s, the radio commercial was firmly established, as was the American system of commercial broadcasting, which provided a natural pattern for television when it appeared on the scene after World War II. Advertisers were, indeed, sponsors of programs. Through their advertising agencies they would often initiate production of a program for the air time they had purchased or, by virtue of being "owners" of a time slot, exercise direct control over the writers, directors and producers of the show.

By the late 1950s, this system of sponsor dominance and network acquiescence was being seriously questioned. The networks responded by assuming greater control over their own programming. In 1960, *Broadcasting* magazine reported that four out of five prime-time shows in the coming season would be licensed to the networks carrying them and subsequently sold to advertisers.

This change, along with rapidly rising program costs, accelerated the move toward selling spots rather than programs. Commercial interruptions became more obvious than in the days when a sponsor might use his allotted time for fewer but longer messages. The problem of commercial "clutter" became more pronounced when further cost escalation, and advertiser demands, led the networks to accept two thirty-second commercials in place of the standard minute.

In addition, the shift to spot buying resulted in a different kind of programming. Audiences were always measured in some fashion, even in radio days, and less popular shows were dropped after a while unless beneficent sponsors wanted to maintain them for purposes of prestige. But spots are priced on the basis of a program's audience, and with participating advertisers instead of sponsors, the Nielsen audience ratings became a matter of deadly seriousness. Networks entered into grim competition for the greatest share of total viewers in each prime-time half-hour. Program schedules were shifted in mid-season, low-rated shows axed without mercy.

The networks' mad race for sheer audience volume set television on a course totally different from that followed by other mass communications media, which have become much less "mass" over the past fifteen years. Radio has all but dropped the idea of networks to concentrate on serving geographical areas. In addition, it has segmented the audience so that one station appeals to "Top 40" fans, another to "All News" listeners, others to "Easy Listening" or "Classical Music" fanciers. Those, in fact, are the designations for the formats used in each market to attract a specific kind of audience to a particular station.

Newspapers have grown more selective, as well. Big city dailies are folding constantly, yet there are more newspapers than ever because new ones are blooming and flourishing in suburban communities, where they provide a more personal service to a smaller but more affluent circulation. At the same time, mass circulation magazines like *Life* and *Look* have given way to specialized interest books like *Sports Illustrated*, *New York* and *National Geographic*.

While all this was happening, television was going for the lowest common denominator with *All in the Family* and *The Love*

Boat. Consequently, advertising people no longer know the individual to whom they're talking in a commercial. More educated, articulate viewers are insulted by humor and situations and language chosen to make sure the least acute won't miss the point. The indiscriminate race for numbers results in men being exposed to vaginal deodorant commercials that embarrass not them but their wives. It results in "Please Don't Squeeze the Charmin" and "Ring Around the Collar" and dozens of other campaigns that sell merchandise to people and make them resent it at the same time. Because they feel, with some justification, that they're being talked down to.

Another damaging event in TV history was the standardization of the thirty-second length for commercials. Where is it written that thirty seconds is the optimum length for any sales message? How could it be equally appropriate for Coca-Cola's reminder spot and Citibank's introductory commercial for a legally complex certificate of deposit? Isn't some dullness or insult to the intelligence bound to ensue, to say nothing of the strain placed on the viewer's patience by the resultant clutter?

Television is different from print and even radio. Those differences make it an extraordinarily effective tool for certain advertising jobs, and that effectiveness has made many in my business reluctant to face the fact that there may be a price to pay in consumer ill will. I happen to believe the effectiveness will be enhanced if the ill will can be diminished. The question is, how?

Well, we can't change the basic nature of the medium, and we can't turn the clock back thirty years and redirect the course of commercial television and television commercials. But if we look to the future with an optimistic eye, certain impending decisions offer opportunities to undo the mistakes of the past. Or, of course, to make them all over again.

At the moment, a number of electronic advances are converging into what the press is calling "the new technologies." This is something of a misnomer, because few of them are really new. Cable television, for example, has been around for more than fifteen years. But the new technologies also include satellite

46

transmission and reception, home videotape and videodisc players, compact computer terminals and other marvels that, if you include what is called "required software," can reasonably be described as new.

While they may sound technical, the new technologies, unless you intend to be a repairman, are really rather simple. It all comes down to this: people will be able to do more things with their TV sets. There will be greater choice than there is today, because information—in its broadest sense—will be available from more sources. And since there will be more sources, there will be a correspondingly greater diversity of audience interest.

In addition to the over-the-air transmissions most of us rely on now, there will be four other conduits of information to our TV screens. One will be cable, which will provide us with many sources of programming. And if it develops as I think it will, those sources will each appeal to a specific interest. The signs already point in that direction.

Another will be two-way cable, through which information can be both received and sent by the individual at the home screen. Two-way cable is actually operating today. Viewers let the sender know, by pushing buttons, what they think about what they're seeing, or they answer specific questions. So the source can be immediately responsive to the audience. What's more, audience interest can be measured.

A third new technique will use satellites to bounce signals to a much greater area than is possible with on-air broadcasting and gather signals from anyone who wants to pay the price. Satellites will provide more sources than most viewers have today, but senders will have no idea who might be receiving, other than that he was willing to pay for a decoder and have a big, ugly dish stuck on his roof. The audience will be a broad, undifferentiated one.

The fourth new technology is videotape recordings and videodiscs. These allow the viewer himself to select not only the source of information but the time of its appearance. This means, of course, that his interest will be total.

Well, so much for technology. What does it have to do with

47

advertising and the implicit contract? Indeed, will advertising be
a part of it? Yes, I believe it will. But the advertising will be
different from what we generally see on our TV screens today.
Some changes will be dictated by the characteristics of the
sources, as just described; some by the kind of interest the
audience brings to them; and some by the fact that advertising
will be unexpected and, like any unexpected guest, will have to
behave itself or be thrown out.

If what U.S. television has represented up to now is "broadcasting," we will soon be entering the age of "narrowcasting."
For an advertiser broadcasting means reaching the largest possible number of people with his message—whether they are legitimate prospects for his brand or not. The concept of broadcasting
explains why so many people see commercials not intended for
them and are often bored, annoyed or even embarrassed by them.

But the inevitable result of more choices will be segmentation.
I believe we'll see channels devoted to special interests: news
and public affairs; entertainment; sports; drama and the arts;
ethnic affairs; children's programs. It happened to magazines. It
happened to radio. Now it can happen to television. And when
it does, an advertiser will know the person he's addressing with
his commercial. He'll know his or her interests, so he can make
the message more involving and important. He'll know how that
person lives and talks, so he can make it more personal. He'll
know what he or she wants, so he can point out more specific and
compelling benefits.

A man I admired greatly, Fairfax Cone, once said, "There is
no such thing as a Mass Mind. The Mass Audience is made up
of individuals, and good advertising is written always from one
person to another. When it is aimed at millions it rarely moves
anyone." In the age of narrowcasting, we'll be able to heed that
advice in a way that is seldom possible on television today.

Two-way cable promises the advertiser some fascinating possibilities, and the most fascinating is direct selling. The experts
predict that at some future date, the viewer will be able to order
the product he's just seen advertised by punching the proper
numbers. His order, his name and address and his charge num-

ber will be electronically processed, and the merchandise immediately sent.

There will be no need, under those circumstances, for copy
testing. Sales will be the measurement rather than adherence to
some weary format. And sales are the ultimate vote of affirmation consumers can provide. Furthermore, when a real consumer, multiplied by millions, can tell us from his living room what
he thought of our commercial—whether or not it was interesting
or believable, whether or not it insulted his taste or intelligence—I
think there will be fewer "Ring Around the Collars" and "Please
Don't Squeeze the Charmins" on the air.

Another promise of two-way cable is the "product information library." By being connected to a home computer terminal
that can order up information on any product category the
prospect might be looking into, the television screen will become
a video catalogue. While we won't know exactly when our
message will reach him, we will know it's going to someone
who's interested and ready to buy. We'll also know he's comparing our sales message, point-by-point, with those of the competition. Only the hopeless among us will be able to bore a
prospect under those circumstances.

These factors alone should lead to fewer breaches of the
contract. But there's still another positive sign. I suspect there
will be no single prescribed length for such product information
commercials. We will buy as much time as is essential to interest
and engage the prospect, to thoroughly inform and attempt to
persuade. Advertiser and viewer will be freed from the tyranny
of the thirty-second spot.

But if a spot in the product information library is "invited,"
some other forms spawned by the new technologies will defi-
nitely not be. As software costs rise, sources that are now characterized by being commercial-free may start including one or
more discreet messages.

Movies and other home entertainments on videotape cassettes
are so expensive due to the cost of the content that bootlegging
has become a sizable underground industry. Aboveground, rental
is more prevalent than purchase. The risk of bootlegging and the

inconvenience of renting will, I predict, open the door to commercial messages. And, though they'd deny it, operators of pay-TV companies are already discussing—albeit very informally—the possibility of selling time for the "right kind" of institutional message.

What is the "right kind"? Obviously it will have to be an exquisitely executed and well-mannered message for a company of recognized quality, a commercial as engaging and rewarding as the program material itself. Perhaps more so, since it will have to win over an audience surprised at encountering advertising in a service sold to them on an ad-free basis. That's a large order. But if it's filled, the quality of television advertising in general will surely improve. And it's not an entirely uncharted course. A few advertisers who bucked the trends by continuing to sponsor and be identified with specific programs have set similar standards for their own commercials. One is Hallmark Cards, with its celebrated *Hallmark Hall of Fame*.

Satellite transmission will probably not be a form of narrowcasting at all. Initially the so-called footprints of the satellites will be geographically confined, but the inevitable temptation will be to broaden the area covered—to saturate an enormous land mass with a program source. The sender will know very little about the receiver. For some senders that may be an acceptable tradeoff for the potentially staggering numbers, but one missing piece of information could be critical: what language does the receiver speak?

Thus far this has not been a serious problem, because the satellite transmissions are picked up only by authorized receiving stations, which then deliver them selectively via cable. But soon decoders and antennae will begin appearing in and on homes. Already a few enterprising TV freaks are picking up everything the satellites are sending with their own dish antennae. Given man's basic compulsion to "beat the system," I suspect he'll find a way around the decoders, too. And soon, like everything else electronic, the size of the rig and its price will diminish.

Then the question of language takes on importance. On the

North American continent, what language do you use in order to sell to English-speaking Americans and Canadians, to Spanish-speaking Mexicans and Americans, and to French-speaking Quebecois? On the European continent the question obviously becomes far more complex—to say nothing of product availability problems and national laws.

One answer may lie in the technology itself. The system predicted for Europe envisions a choice of two or three different channels offering the same picture with different sound tracks (strangely enough, if people are speaking on camera, the maximum verisimilitude in synchronizing voice to lip movement is achieved by shooting the original version in Dutch). It is more likely, in my view, that satellite commericals will diminish the reliance on verbal communication and lean more heavily on graphics. And this shift will improve the quality of commercials immensely.

Television is primarily a visual medium. The most effective and best-remembered commercials in the brief history of TV have been essentially visual: the Timex torture tests, a chimpanzee making Xerox copies, the tiger in the tank. Recently commercials, particularly U.S. commercials, have become walls of words. As many words are packed in as possible. And I believe this contributes to the charge of dullness. If the undifferentiated audience for satellite transmission forces a renewed concentration on visual selling, both the viewer and the advertiser will benefit.

I may be placing too much hope in the new technologies—optimism is endemic in advertising people—but I don't think so. The technological changes I described in the medium are already realities. The qualitative changes I predict in the message are likely to come about simply because they will make television advertising more effective and will therefore be spurred by the force of dollars.

These developments will not magically endear all television commercials to the American heart overnight. The sequential nature of the medium will always produce some degree of resentment. Violations of the implicit contract will remain a temptation for some. But for a society that in a recent survey expressed the belief that Americans will generally be less well off in the future than today, this view of a more welcome species of television commercial ahead may provide a small element of cheer.

THE BASIC NATURE OF ADVERTISING

On almost every television talk show on which I've appeared, some professor or consumerist or pale new author is bound to jab a finger at me and deliver this line with grave finality: "You sell people things they don't need."

My only response is "Of course I do. So do you." People *need* very little other than food, water and shelter. The richness of human life, as opposed to that of the beasts, is largely a result of things we don't need at all. Pope Julius II didn't *need* to have the ceiling of his chapel painted by Michelangelo. The people of Chartres didn't *need* a cathedral.

On a more mundane scale, people do not *need* automobiles, refrigerators, books, blue jeans or toothpaste. But they *want* these things. They want even more frivolous items such as hair color, potato chips, antiperspirants, chewing gum, perfume and jewelry. Frail creatures that we are, we want things that make our lives easier, happier, pleasanter, more promising or even longer. And from time immemorial we have been selling such things to one another. Yes, I sell people things they don't need. I can't, however, sell them something they don't want. Even with advertising. Even if I were of a mind to.

I am tired of such sorties from the camp of those who refuse to see advertising as simply salesmanship functioning in the paid space and time of mass communication media. I am equally tired of arguments from those who do recognize it as such but believe that freedom of choice, which underlies the concept, is too heady a privilege to extend to the bumbling American consumer.

I am tired of both because I think they are attempts to

change the basic nature of things. Buying and selling—or at least trading—are so much a part of all societies past and present that the practice and all its conventions must be imprinted somewhere in our genes. The use of existing forms of communication to expedite and broaden the process has been common since the days of clay tablets and papyrus. The basic right of individuals to dispose of their drachmas or dollars for whatever object, sublime or ridiculous, is inherent in the system.

Interfere with this simple natural order and mischief ensues. Throughout history there have been groups motivated by ambition, greed or an odd sense of divine guidance who stuck clumsy fingers into the flawed but functioning system to the detriment of all. Fixing the price of bread ridiculously low in eighteenth-century France, thus driving *boulangers* out of business and assuring no bread at all, cost Louis XVI and Marie Antoinette dearly, whether or not she really responded, "Let them eat cake." Prohibition in America was hardly a resounding success.

If Dante had allowed me to make assignments to the lowest rings of hell, I would have issued tickets to all those who meddle with things that are working and try to turn them into something they weren't intended to be. Included in that group would be those who demand that advertising be journalism. And those who diguise political campaigning as advertising. And those who would deny anyone the right to spend his last dollar on a six-pack of Michelob if he so chose.

Paradise, on the other hand, would have plush accommodations for all who value and protect those things that function and endure, who diligently perform their tasks to the best of their abilities, who devote their additional energy and creativity to improving the machinery and eliminating its flaws.

Having thus separated the goats from the sheep, I will now try to look at my craft with an eye toward making it work better for the latter group—the righteous, the consumers. I do this for no altruistic reason. My motivation is the same fuel that propels everyone else and everything else in the system: my own well-being. The better advertising works, the more effective and efficient it will become, and the more money advertisers will spend on it.

Consumers understand this. They understand the natural order of things. That's why they accept the implicit contract. Sam Goldwyn once said, "A verbal contract isn't worth the paper it's printed on." That makes an implicit contract very fragile, indeed. It is important to guard against violations of that contract, deliberate or inadvertent, that would result in consumers losing faith in advertising generally. They, after all, are living up to their end admirably.

PART II

*What goes
down the elevator
determines
what goes
up the flagpole.*

ADVERTISING PEOPLE

You may have heard the statement Fairfax Cone once made about the advertising agency business: "The inventory goes down the elevator every night." Actually it's far more than the inventory. It's the production plant, the sales force and the management. It's also the quality control department.

An advertising agency is nothing but people. The advertiser supplies the raw material: marketing problems. The media provide the distribution system. The people who are an advertising agency make the messages. The quality of those messages depends totally on the quality of the people themselves and the attitudes about their craft that they bring to each task.

Of course, their success and the rewards they receive hang on the effectiveness of the messages they create—effectiveness measured in terms of accomplishing the advertiser's objectives. In their eagerness for success, a misguided few assume that results are more speedily attained by lying, misleading, boring or talking down to the consumer. They are wrong. Real advertising effectiveness cannot be achieved by violating the contract. It's quite the other way around.

Thus it is imperative that people who go into advertising understand, first of all, what it is and what it isn't. It's imperative that they understand the spirit and all the clauses of the implicit contract under which they will be dealing with the consumer. And it is imperative that they are born with or learn or have pounded into their heads the proper attitudes about the craft they are privileged to practice.

Too many go into advertising for the wrong reasons. People whose interests and talents are clearly directed to business and marketing but who feel no fascination with the process of mass communication have no place in an advertising agency. They belong in a manufacturing or sales company. Similarly, people who burn with the need to communicate and love to tinker with communication tools will not succeed if they disdain or lack interest in business and marketing. They belong in a studio or a writer's garret.

The people I know who have done well in advertising agencies have, without exception, been good at and most often obsessed with both aspects of the field. One interest may precede the other; an artist may be born with communicative talents and develop a zest for business later. One may exceed the other; this is why some go into copywriting while others choose account management or research or media work. But one can never replace the other.

These people have other characteristics in common. They are fascinated with human behavior: what makes us tick, how we act and react in groups and in a society. They have an unquenchable thirst to find out why people do what they do, to plumb the enigma of their infinite individuality and essential similarity, to get out and listen to them and understand them—even the ones very different from themselves. I've never known a successful advertising person who wasn't a closet social psychologist.

Successful advertising people are also compulsive communicators. They've done a lot of writing simply because they had something that needed saying—or taken photographs or drawn drawings because there were images that had never been seen from quite that point of view before. Early on they knew they had to get their thoughts, feelings and ideas before others. Most, therefore, are quite verbal, though not always in terms of the spoken word. A number of fine advertising men I've known have had severe stuttering problems but superb writing skills. Some others, articulate and eloquent, couldn't write worth a damn. Those who aren't verbal are avid graphic communicators, and a few satisfy the compulsion through music.

Given these not insubstantial qualities, these highly marketable personality quirks, what environmental influences would lead such people into as small and unsung a world as the advertising agency? Maybe an answer or two will emerge in looking at the events that directed one life toward Madison Avenue. It's the only life I can sift through with impunity and in which I can isolate influences with any certainty.

AN ADVERTISING PERSON

There were only two things in my life that I am sure did nothing to direct me toward a career in advertising. In fact, they pointed me in the opposite direction. They were called Principles of Advertising and Advertising Copywriting.

The school of journalism that, however reluctantly, awarded me a degree required students to take several courses outside their field of concentration. Mine being news-editorial, I elected the aforementioned courses in the advertising sequence, a sequence that we "real journalists" looked upon with open disdain.

As for Principles of Advertising, I did not at the time, nor do I now, understand what the professor was talking about. His discussion of layout dynamics based on "torque and vector" principles must have been some sort of cosmic insight visited upon him alone. On the other hand, I understood very well what the instructor of Advertising Copywriting was up to. Having once worked in an agency, he would regale his students with tales of neckties being snipped off with scissors, of tasteless clients and lovable drunks. Then he'd give an assignment that was graded, it appeared, on the student's prowess in obscuring the product benefit with a pun.

By the end of the quarter, which was the final quarter of my senior year, it was clear I would get a D, which in Journalism was tantamount to flunking the course. This meant no degree, since at the time the Chinese were doing rude things to the U.S. Eighth Army in Korea and I was faced with being drafted or enlisting; coming back to repeat Advertising Copywriting did not seem to fit my government's plans. Swept away with patriotic fervor, the instructor gave me a C-minus, and I completed what was necessary to graduate from Northwestern University's Medill School of Journalism.

There's an epilogue to the saga of the copywriting instructor, which reveals the mischievousness of the gods and the pettiness of man. Six years later he applied for a job at Foote, Cone & Belding in Chicago. My copy chief, knowing I had been at Medill when the luckless fellow was teaching there, came in and asked me about him. A bigger man would probably have said, "I was really in no position to judge. Why not give him a try?" Instead, as I recall, I said, "He's not a bad guy. But if you're talking about advertising, one of us couldn't tell an ad from his ass."

I left Northwestern in December 1950. The degree itself was awarded in June 1951, when my class officially graduated. It was sent to me at the U.S. Marine Corps Recruit Training Depot, Parris Island, South Carolina, and handed to me at mail call by my drill instructor. Knowing his lack of reverence for higher education, I'm grateful he didn't realize what was in the envelope.

So much for the contributions of academe to my preparation for advertising. Far more important were the twists of fate or chromosomal structure that seemed always to involve me with, and increase my regard for, mass communications.

When someone asks me what I am—as opposed to what I do—I say, "A writer." I always have. I don't know when it started, but I clearly remember when it began to make a difference. When I was fifteen, a family friend took one of the verses I'd written, a flawed quatrain sequence about the gold and russet beauty of autumn, and sent it to the *Chicago Tribune*'s column "In the Wake of the News." A week or so later I was astonished to see my poem—to say nothing of my name—in glorious ten-point type.

Soon I was turning poems out faster than the editor wanted them. I began sending some to a *Chicago Sun-Times* writer named Dale Harrison, who used a poem now and then in his column, "Top of the Town." But what I really had my eye on was a column entitled "A Line o' Type or Two," edited by Charles

Collins, which appeared on the editorial page of the *Tribune*. This was the truly prestigious place for poets to appear, the standards being high enough to attract some who were being published in literary magazines.

With a poem running about once a week over my name in two lesser columns, I realized Mr. Collins might not welcome O'Toole and his works, however worthy, to his distinguished column. So I made up a name, one so lyrical and WASP that no one would suspect there was an Irish Catholic lad from the South Side lurking behind it. Thus did Elliot Carter arrive in Chicago and begin appearing in "A Line o' Type or Two" with a frequency that irritated a few other contributors. About a year later I met Charles Collins and confessed all, but by that time I had stopped sending poems to the other two columns and was exclusively Elliot Carter. In the neighborhood where I grew up there was a certain peril in being known as a poet. The *nom de plume* was the better part of valor.

Charles Collins proved to be a good friend as well as a fine and literate gentleman. After recovering from the jarring discovery that the pet poet in his stable was a skinny seventeen-year-old kid, he became my advisor. He guided me from Loyola University, where I spent my freshman year, to Northwestern University and the Medill School of Journalism. Furthermore, he helped me select some verses from the hundred or so he had published, find a printer and in 1947 publish a small volume titled *The Days of Wine and Roses* (I was not the last to lift that phrase from Ernest Dowson). As a result of the publicity the book received in "A Line o' Type or Two," the profit was enough to pay my first year's tuition at Northwestern.

This absorption in poetry, which continued over the years with an occasional appearance in obscure magazines, was immensely helpful in adapting to the disciplines of advertising writing. Synthesis of conception, economy of expression, the lyricism that contributes to memorability—these skills that are so essential to good advertising are the basic tools of the poet.

During my last year in high school I landed a part-time job as an usher at the CBS Radio outlet in Chicago known as WBBM.

THE TROUBLE WITH ADVERTISING . . .

An usher in a radio station might seem an anomaly now, but in 1946 a number of radio shows were still played before a live audience. My job was to line the eager fans up so that I might take their tickets, then guide them to their seats in the ample studio-theater where they would watch actors and announcers stand around microphones and read scripts.

Despite the lack of physical "theater," despite the unprepossessing character of the actors before air time, I would stand entranced at the rear of the darkened studio as Barbara Luddy and Olan Soulé wove an engaging little *First Nighter* playlet out of nothing but words, voices and sound effects. I would shiver inside my blue and gold uniform as Everett Clarke, playing "The Whistler," spun another tale of terror and bizarre occurrences.

After the audience and the actors had gone, I would go up on the stage to retrieve a discarded script, which I would take home and study. I had to find out how the writer constructed the plot to fall into acts, how he alternated dialogue and narration to achieve certain effects with each, how he chose the words that created such clearly defined scenes in "the theater of the mind." And I would read the scripts aloud, trying to recall the inflections with which those marvelous actors had added another dimension to the words themselves.

Thus I was prepared when serendipity struck in 1948. Since I arrived at Northwestern with only my tuition money, the problem of eating remained. I needed a job. Walking through the School of Speech one day, I spotted a notice on the bulletin board stating that a slot was open on the announcing staff of the Evanston FM station, WEAW. Auditions would be held the following Saturday morning.

I arrived at the station early that icy morning to find at least fifty speech students ahead of me. Soon there were another fifty behind me. All of them were conversing in mellifluous tones, their magnificent voices reverberating throughout the tiny reception room. My heart sank. I got through my audition somehow and went back to my rented room with the distinct feeling that I had made a fool of myself. A week later I received a letter telling me I had the job. Subsequently I learned that I was the only one who had pronounced both Modest Moussorgsky and Jawaharlal Nehru correctly.

I sometimes think no one should be allowed to write copy for an announcer without having been one himself. No one who has ever labored before a microphone would overburden an announcer with more words than can reasonably be fitted into the allotted time, thus creating a frenzied and less than persuasive race for the finish line. Nor would he fail to provide for those slight pauses that can often say more than words, or overlook colorful and active words that limn vivid pictures in the imagination. Every announcer who has ever had to record a piece of my copy has benefitted from that year I spent doing classical music and news shows, church services and interviews, late-night disc-jockey gigs and thousands of commercials at "WEAW, serving Chicago and Northern Illinois from Evanston . . . 101.5 on your FM dial."

To return for a moment to my days as an usher at WBBM, the word got out among the people there that the punk in the uniform wrote poetry. Some, indeed, were among the small and odd following Elliot Carter had somehow attracted. One afternoon after the crowd had departed, enriched by an episode of *Those Websters*, I was visited in the basement locker room, where ushers exchanged their uniforms for their own drab garments, by two unique gentlemen with an idea that was even more unique.

One was a portly fellow, thirty or so years old, with black hair a good deal longer than was customary in those days. I had never before seen anyone wear his coat as a cape, not putting his arms through the sleeves. Despite the venerable spots and stains on the coat itself, I was intrigued. His name was Bruno Visoto, and he described himself as a producer of radio and theatrical drama. He introduced his companion, a somewhat older man with a magnificent profile and the obvious impediment of an artificial leg, as "the actor George Mitchell." As the two of them wove the ornate tapestry of their idea in that sterile locker room in the bowels of the Wrigley Building, my eyes widened and my world along with them. I was going into television!

It seems that the Zenith Radio Company and Balaban and Katz had recently opened an experimental television station in Chicago called WBKB. Despite the fact that they were broadcasting little more than test patterns and wrestling matches, they had a vast library of film and still photographs. And they were hungering for program ideas. We were going to scour that library for material of artistic worth, I was going to write poetry to go with it, George was going to read it over the visuals, and Bruno was going to direct and produce the whole thing. It would be a weekly program called *Momentary Moods*. And we would all become famous.

The incredible thing is that all of it happened. Except the last.

The show was a five-minute segment that opened with the title and with recorded music that went under as George's glorious profile dissolved on in silhouette. As he removed the prop pipe from his mouth and began reading my swollen, sugary verse, film clips of lonely trains racing across bleak countrysides or snowflakes descending on Grant Park were interspersed with stills of lovely, haunted girls or couples walking hand in hand through enchanted forests. Back to the profile, roll the credits, and fade to black.

Although *Momentary Moods* lasted only four weeks, I learned much about television in that jammed and rudimentary studio in Chicago. Amidst snakelike cables and sweaty confusion, I found out what a camera can and cannot do and what marvels can be performed on the control console.

More important, I learned something about audience response. Wanting to see the show on a television set, I went one evening to the only place where such treasures could be found in those days: a local bar. I ordered a Coke and persuaded the bartender to turn on the set five minutes before the wrestling match to see a program I knew he and his patrons would find interesting. It was, I think, about thirty seconds after George's profile gave way to autumn leaves and the splendor of my words that the laughter mounted to such a crescendo that the bartender turned the sound off. Somehow I knew we weren't going to last more than four weeks.

But all of these ventures into the beguiling world of mass communications, however instructive, taught me less of subsequent value than some other jobs I had.

When I was twelve I sold *Liberty* magazine door-to-door. At thirteen I got a secondhand bicycle and, thus mechanized, took on a delivery route for the *Chicago Daily News*. I can still see those housewives eagerly opening the magazine and beginning to read before I was able to make change, and the old men shuffling out to pick up the paper as quickly as my unerring arm lofted it onto their porches. What those publications brought into their lives was precious to them. And the fact that I had few difficulties collecting what they owed, in what was hardly an affluent neighborhood at the tail end of the Depression, attests to something I still tell publishers today: the magazine and the newspaper are the best value for the money in this whole mercantile society.

The Medill School of Journalism was filled when I applied in 1947, and despite the best efforts of Charles Collins and his comrades at the *Tribune*, I had to wait until the beginning of the winter quarter, January 1948, to enter. This gave me six months, from the conclusion of classes at Loyola in June, to fill with some sort of gainful activity. I spent the evenings writing: poems, some for "A Line o' Type or Two" and others for magazines; and short stories, one of which I sold to the *Sun-Times*. The days I spent at a job that was, on the surface, a rather mindless activity but that gave me insights I still find valuable. I worked for the Commonwealth Edison Company as a meter reader.

Each morning I would be given a book with the name, address and meter number of everyone in a designated area who was a customer of the electric utility. I would write down the numbers appearing on the meter and subtract the previous month's reading, thereby providing my employer with the number of kilowatt-hours used by that family. A day's work involved reading about two hundred meters, of which some were outside but most were found in basements, back staircases and sometimes bedrooms. All day long I went in and out of people's homes, seeing what they surrounded themselves with, smelling what they cooked, feeling how they lived.

At the first of the month our crew would begin at Thirty-ninth Street, the blackest and toughest part of the city, and by the end of the month we would have worked our way out to the southernmost reaches of affluent Morgan Park and the steel mill communities along Lake Michigan. In six months I visited every home and apartment building on the South Side of Chicago. I suspect no other advertising agency chairman can make that statement.

And what richly diverse cultures were represented in each month's southward trek. There were the black ghettos where smoky music snaked from dim, foul-smelling rooms and each day I walked through several of the illegal numbers games that brought joy to the unemployed who gathered in those dank basements. There was the Jewish enclave around the University of Chicago, where I saw black-clad men with long curls and wondered if it was a sin to enter a temple just for meter-reading purposes. Over west was the huge Polish community of spotless homes redolent with warm cooking odors, where women in kerchiefs came home from shopping with live geese peering out from wicker baskets. South of that was Little Lithuania, where the pale-eyed, honey-haired girls coming home from high school brought an ache to my heart. And around West Englewood there was an Italian area where the air in the tiny grocery stores sang with the rich aroma emanating from giant wheels of parmesan cheese and, in the language spoken by old men with thick moustaches, I thought I caught the iambic rhythms of Dante.

I learned that Chicago was less a real entity than were the neighborhoods it comprised. And so, I began to suspect, was America. I learned that people are essentially nice, decent people, each in his own way (I could not, however, say the same for their dogs). I reflect on those pilgrimages through the various Chicagos whenever I get the feeling that affluence or incipient sophistication or just the narrowing influence of midtown Manhattan is giving me emotional sclerosis. No matter the passage of time, those people are the prospects for our clients' products today—far more so than the fellows on the platform at the Greenwich station or the women one might meet at a cocktail party at the Museum of Modern Art.

During the last two summers of my career at Northwestern, I had another job that enriched my understanding of communications by broadening my understanding of the people who are the audience. I conducted groups of tourists from Chicago to various points around North America for a company called Happiness Tours—a name that produced such acute embarrassment within me that I carried their briefcase so that the logotype was always facing my leg. Aside from that, it was a rewarding job in many ways.

In each Chicago railroad station there was a Happiness Tours desk where, on the appointed day, I would greet my new charges. We would then board a train for a two- or three-week tour of Colorado; or Grand Canyon, Los Angeles and San Francisco; or Niagara Falls, New York City and Washington; or the deluxe package consisting of Jasper Park, Lake Louise, Banff and Glacier Park. The fact that I was innocent of any previous experience with these places didn't seem to bother my employer. But I felt obliged to stay up all night reading about each destination so that I could feign some familiarity as I wearily stepped off the train in the morning. ("Oh, yes. That's Pikes Peak over there, 14,110 feet above sea level.")

The tours varied considerably in size. I took a group of 49 to the Canadian Rockies one summer. Another time I had 114 to shepherd through the complexities of Manhattan and Washington. Since, in the latter case, 101 of them were female, you can imagine the gratuitous comments I received as I led them across Times Square one evening.

The tourists were from everywhere in the Midwest. They were teachers, clerks, factory workers and small businessmen. They were families, single people, widows and widowers. Their common bond was a desire to travel in the company of others, either because of shyness or because of gregariousness.

They were fascinating. I grew genuinely fond of almost every one. Even when they'd call me at two in the morning to tell me the toilet in their room wouldn't flush.

These, too, are the people I think about when I'm looking at an ad or commercial before it goes to the client: good, hardworking people who are interested in life and enjoy a good time; insecure and defensive at first, but warm and open when they get to know you; people with sense and sensibilities that an advertiser cannot violate for very long with impunity. They are American consumers.

After leaving the idyllic lakeside campus of Northwestern University and its renowned school of journalism, I enlisted in the Marine Corps. Following boot camp I was commissioned and at last had a real, full-time job: infantry platoon commander. I am hard pressed to find many ways in which this job prepared me for advertising, although there have been times when basic survival techniques have been useful.

I spent a year in Korea and, upon returning, was released from active duty. Thus, in early 1953, I was an ex-marine, ex-radio announcer, ex-meter reader, ex-tour-conducting poet with a degree in journalism and some experience in waiting on tables, washing dishes and writing television continuity. Where else would I look for a paying job but in an advertising agency?

AN ADVERTISING AGENCY

I don't like those ads in the back of certain magazines that promise some poor, loveless girl larger mammary glands in a matter of weeks, because I know they're lies. And because I think they annoy people, I don't like commercials in which two women—one dominant and articulate, the other uncertain and searching—stand in a kitchen or supermarket saying things no humans ever said to one another, talking in slogans, until the weaker has been totally convinced that the product will save her ailing marriage or make her children love her. This format, by the way, is referred to by the cynical mercenaries who rely on it as "Two C's in a K." The "K" stands for kitchen. I'll leave the meaning of the "C's" to your imagination.

I don't like advertising that depicts consumers as fools, that shouts, that offends general standards of taste, that relies on racial or ethnic stereotypes or perpetuates the concept that women were created solely to wash dishes and clothes, to satisfy man's sexual urges and to bear babies. Had I ever been coerced into making advertising like this, I would now be in the city room of some newspaper or, perhaps, back conducting tours or reading meters. I'm happy this never occurred, because despite the above, I happen to love advertising.

Mass communication, it seems to me, is the dominating force and the defining characteristic of our times. Geopolitics is still a factor, but the ultimate step in geopolitics is war. And the ultimate type of war has thus far been avoided because the peoples of the world are aware, through mass communication, of its inevitable result. Even a limited war in Vietnam was forced to a conclusion by the national revulsion of a society that for the first time in history had the unspeakable reality brought into its living rooms through mass communication.

The communications explosion and the technological explosion that followed World War II are often seen as identical. In fact they are quite different developments, each with different roots and frequently with different purposes. In our country we've seen consumerism and environmentalism employ mass communication to close down businesses and limit or wipe out entire industries. Our century will, I'm convinced, be remembered by historians not as another phase of the technological boom but as the beginning of the communications explosion. There can be no more exciting field in which to earn one's daily bread.

Nor is utilizing the fruits of this explosion to facilitate the mass distribution of goods and services any less important and worthy than employing them to distribute entertainment or information. We have constructed a system in this country by which it is possible to deliver the same message to 200,000,000 people in the same language at the same time. It is an astonishing reality, unparalleled in history or in any other part of today's world. Using the capabilities of this system to perform the selling function that was done on a one-by-one basis throughout our mercantile history has made our physical lives easier and better.

We have tools and clothing, transportation and sports equipment, air conditioners and heaters, stereos and cameras—thousands of things that many of us would not be able to afford were it not for the economies brought about by mass distribution through mass communication. We are better nourished because of the food products this system brings to our attention, we have better teeth than our predecessors because advertising taught us to brush them, and many of us are healthier because advertising told us about low-calorie foods and beverages.

All of this has not been without its attendant problems. But then, with anything as highly visible as advertising, there is no scarcity of people to point out the problems as they become apparent. And so far there has been no demonstrated inability of the system to solve each problem with reasonable dispatch.

So, for anyone who feels compelled to be involved in something of both immediate and historical importance, who isn't afraid of the perils presented by a high profile, who is in awe of the power and potential of mass communication, who is equally enamored of newspapers, magazines, radio and television, who is fascinated by the behavior of people both individually and as a society—advertising is the only place to be. But he had better bring to it the right set of attitudes. And have the good fortune I had in finding an agency that shared them and an employer like Fairfax Cone.

I went to work for Mr. Cone in Chicago in 1954. And it was truly more to work for him than for Foote, Cone & Belding that I left another agency after a year's apprenticeship. Fax, at that time, was a dominant figure in advertising and in the Chicago community, and his fame, as well as his rather stern appearance, veiled a gentle, aesthetic and shy nature. He had started out as an art director but soon wearied of the deception required to hide his darkest secret: he was color-blind. So he turned to copywriting, a trade he never abandoned. He was widely known in the business as a man who was serious about it, who abhorred its excesses and took pride in its accomplishments, who exhibited little patience with dilettantes, and who knew what he was doing. I figured if I was going to spend most of my waking hours at this craft, I should learn it from someone like that.

The day I met him he was being presented with a watch commemorating his twenty-fifth year with the company. He had started the year I was born. I remember him saying that day, "I hope you like it here." That was twenty-eight years ago. I guess I did.

For the next eleven years I saw a good deal of Fax Cone. Later, after returning to Chicago from a two-year stint in Los Angeles, I spent even more time with him. As a copywriter, as a supervisor, as a copy group head, as creative director, I would take my work and that of my writers and art directors to him seeking his approval. We talked about it, we argued about it, we changed it and we rechanged it. We talked. I learned. I would revel in his highest compliment, "Damn good." I would dread his sternest rebuke, "Would you say that to someone you know?"

But the conversation would frequently range far from advertising. Knowing my interest in poetry, he would initiate discussions of poets whose work he had read in the *New Yorker*. Soon we would be on to history, social psychology, baseball—a subject about which I was clearly ignorant—fiction and film, art and archeology, politics and pretty girls. Fax read more than any man I'd ever met. The bookshelves in his office library were groaning under the weight of more books about advertising than I knew existed. And when I saw the immense and varied library he kept in his apartment on Astor Street, I lusted. It was about that time I began to realize that the proper study of advertising is mankind.

Fax was a man of fine taste and judgment. Sometimes to a fault. I remember how he set off on the only trip to Europe I can recall his taking (it was a sea voyage—he detested flying) with the intention of buying a Rolls-Royce (which his chauffeur would operate—he also detested driving). He came back instead with a Bentley, which, while practically as expensive as a Rolls, was in his judgment a little less ostentatious. Then he had it repainted a slightly darker shade of gray so it would be less flashy.

But he displayed no such reticence in evaluating a layout, his eyes traversing it in search of that balance, that harmony, that flow that invites the reader in and escorts him effortlessly through the elements in exactly the sequence intended. He would point unerringly at any element, device or decoration that was superfluous or just marginally necessary. Simplicity and unity were what he sought in the look of an ad or commercial, and simplicity and clarity were what he constantly demanded of the words. If you get it down to its simplest, most essential elements, that's when creativity occurs; creativity is not something that's applied like frosting. This was what he was forever trying to show us.

Such were the standards he set for himself and for others that few competitive agencies seemed to measure up in his eyes. He had a high regard for Leo Burnett, Young & Rubicam, Ogilvy

& Mather, Doyle Dane Bernbach and several others. But the works of agencies like Ted Bates, Grey and William Esty he found difficult to praise. And the one-liner, sight-gag, rib-tickling hilarity that poured forth from the "boutiques" of the 1960s put him into a rage.

He had a rich and wry sense of humor, nonetheless. He used to come back from meetings with Chicago's formidable Richard J. Daley savoring the mayor's latest malapropism. One of the choicest was "This city is going to rise to higher and higher platitudes of achievement." But he felt that advertising was not the appropriate place to display one's sense of the absurd.

Fax used to put out memos to the organization known, because of the blue band across the top bearing his indecipherable signature, as "Blue Streaks." He made plain in these essays his opinion of the "belly laugh" and "camp humor" schools of advertising. He excoriated magazines for their excesses and particularly lambasted television networks for what he saw as a rapid deterioration in program quality.

Fax once suggested that networks adopt what he called the "magazine concept" of scheduling advertising. With this plan, advertisers would buy a thirteen-week nighttime schedule on a network, and their commercials would rotate through time segments and days of the week. The advertiser would have no more control over what programs his commercial appeared during than a magazine advertiser has over what editorial feature his ad adjoins. Thus there would be advertising support for programs of exceptional quality and low ratings, and advertisers would have no justification to interfere in program content. Each advertiser's message would fall into both high- and low-rated shows, but everything would balance out in the end. The networks, of course, called Cone naive and misguided. I wonder if today, with everyone, including government, exercised about the violence and banality characterizing network programming, they don't wish they had considered his proposal more seriously.

Since he was nothing if not outspoken about his concerns, Fax was not loved by all. *Time* once referred to him as "the scold of the advertising business." But he was respected. Among other honors, he was elected chairman of the American Association of Advertising Agencies. He was chosen Man of the Year by the trade publication, *Advertising Age*, and he was placed in the industry's Hall of Fame. None of these things ever meant as much to him as becoming chairman of the University of Chicago's Board of Trustees.

Fax retired in 1970 to Windswept, the beautiful house he and his wife Gertrude had built. It overlooks the sea and just about everything else in Carmel, California. He died there in June 1977.

In 1964 I was sent to FCB/Los Angeles as creative director. I missed the times with Fax and missed having his judgment to fall back on. But I sent him a lot of our ads and commercials and would always receive a thoughtful critique, often even a "Damn good." And during my years there I noticed something remarkable. The people who worked at FCB/Los Angeles were more like the people at FCB/Chicago than they were like people at other Los Angeles agencies. The approach to the craft, the sensitivity to the reality of the consumer's life, were echoes of the attitudes I had learned from Fax, despite the fact that his years on the Coast were spent in his own San Francisco, not in Southern California. Later, working at FCB/New York and visiting our operations in San Francisco, London, Italy, Germany and elsewhere, I was struck by the same similarities.

So I slowly began to discover that there was more to Foote, Cone & Belding than one man, remarkable as he might be. I started reading some books I should have read long before: books about the original company, Lord & Thomas; books about and by Albert Lasker, who headed it for so many years before turning it over, at the end of 1942, to Emerson Foote, Fairfax Cone and Don Belding, who were running the three geographic divisions; books by the people who turned space brokerage into a communications craft.

In 1873 an advertising agency named Lord & Brewster was founded in the downtown area of the burly city of Chicago. Like the few others that existed at the time (the large ones being J. Walter Thompson and N. W. Ayer), it was not an agency in today's sense of the term. It was a space brokerage house, purchasing space from newspapers and magazines and reselling it to advertisers for the purpose of "keeping their name before the public."

Quite soon the name was changed to Lord & Thomas after the two principals, D. M. Lord and Ambrose Thomas. Both men had come west from Maine. Lord, the older of the two, wore white muttonchop whiskers and a wing collar. He handled the financial and business side. Thomas was a more robust fellow who sported a nicely trimmed moustache and a gold watch chain complete with elk's tooth. He was the advertising partner. Within twenty-five years the two of them built their partnership into the third largest agency in America, just behind Thompson and Ayer, with billings of $800,000 a year (today FCB bills more than a billion dollars). But the smartest move Lord and Thomas made in their business careers occurred in 1898 when they hired, for the sum of $10 a week, an eighteen-year-old lad named Albert D. Lasker, just up from Galveston, Texas.

Lasker had come to Chicago to talk with Lord & Thomas at the insistence of his father. His intention was to spend a few weeks with the firm, then return to Texas and the newspaper business he loved. He left Lord & Thomas forty-four years later, having made something like $50,000,000 in the meantime. One reason he stayed on longer was that, upon arriving in Chicago, he lost $500 to some rather rough characters in a crap game. Since he had only $75 to his name, he talked Mr. Thomas into advancing him the enormous sum and allowing him to pay it back at $2 per week. That, in effect, indentured him for some time.

Lasker was a unique physical presence. John Gunther, who wrote his biography, *Taken at the Flood*, gives this description of the Lasker he first met in 1942. "He was a tall man, taut, very straight and slim; he never had a weight problem, because his nervous energy burned off surplus calories; he was constantly in motion, tense—almost vibrating. He was an extraordinarily warm person, with a passionate love of life, full of curiosity, as eager

78

and enthusiastic as a child. He gave out a spark, a glow. You could almost see his face in the dark." One female friend said, "People looked at him and were no longer lonely."

Fairfax Cone had worked for him for twelve years but didn't meet him until 1941, when Lasker summoned him from San Francisco to Palm Springs to begin the persuasion process that ended with Fax moving to New York. This is what he saw:

> Although his height was no more than average, Albert Lasker seemed taller than most men. His carriage was erect. His strong face, with its aristocratic, aquiline nose, was framed in soft, gray-white hair combed to rise and billow like a short mane toward the back. His eyes were dark and very bright. His blue suit jacket was cut and pressed so that the lapels dipped narrowly to the lowermost button, accentuating the vertical; and I learned all his clothes were made this way. His shirt was plain white and his necktie plain blue. He wore exquisite shoes; exquisite because his feet were very small. When Albert Lasker appeared at the door of his suite, I knew I was in a presence.

My favorite Lasker story tells of his going out to solicit the advertising account of a Midwestern baron who had turned Lord & Thomas people away after several serious presentations. He came back with the business. When asked how he did it, Lasker said, "I simply told the gentleman I was going to make him rich."

Gunther characterized Lasker as "a restless genius." Certainly he involved himself in more activities than most men could fit into five lifetimes. He was controlling owner of the Chicago Cubs baseball team; he was chairman of the U.S. Shipping Board under President Harding; he was a trustee of the University of Chicago; he assembled what is generally acknowledged to be one of the finest collections of French Impressionist paintings in the world; he and his wife, Mary, reorganized and revitalized the Planned Parenthood Association and the American Cancer

Society and established the Lasker Foundation, an organization that funds scores of medical research projects and recognizes distinguished accomplishments in medicine with a coveted award and welcome cash.

But first and foremost, and despite his disillusionment with the craft in his later years, Lasker was an advertising man. He changed advertising from simply a means of "keeping your name before the public" to the mass selling of products and services through mass communication. All his other achievements notwithstanding, he is remembered primarily as "the father of modern advertising."

In 1908, Lasker hired a shy, mousy man who spoke with a lisp and who was, at the time, writing mostly patent medicine ads. The starting salary was an astounding $185,000 a year. The writer's name was Claude Hopkins. Hopkins peers out at us now from ancient photographs with twinkling eyes behind narrow-rimmed spectacles, anything but imposing. But in the context of the craft he practiced, he was a genuine genius. His two books, *Scientific Advertising* and *My Life in Advertising*, remain to this day the most important and influential statements on the subject.

He was forty-one years old when he joined Lord & Thomas. His childhood had been spent in the little Michigan town where he was born and where his father was a minister. He came from a long line of ministers, so the fundamentalist tone of his prose may not be accidental. Hopkins aspired to the pulpit himself, but the family was poor; though he began working at the age of nine, they couldn't save enough to send him to college. This may explain the penuriousness for which he was noted later in life. Despite his unheard-of-salary, he refused to pay more than $6.50 for a pair of shoes.

Hopkins's background may also account for his enormous industry. He usually worked until midnight, often until two in the morning. Sundays, he said, were his most productive days. His inability to go to college must have left some kind of psychic scar, for he often made it known that in his opinion, a college graduate couldn't write a decent ad. "Higher education," he said, "appears to me a handicap to a man whose lifetime work consists in appealing to common people."

By the time he and Lasker met, Hopkins had scored a number of successes, first with the Bissell Carpet Sweeper Company while still in his teens, then as advertising manager of Swift & Co., then with Dr. Shoop's Restorative, a patent medicine for which he produced, as he later wrote, "a class of advertising of which I no longer approve." Lasker's interest in Hopkins was piqued by the campaign he did for Schlitz beer, in which he made a point of the fact that Schlitz cleaned its bottles with "live steam." Other brewers did the same, but Hopkins preempted the claim for Schlitz, thereby leaving competitors reluctant to mention it for fear of looking like followers. For that campaign, he wrote the signature line "The beer that made Milwaukee famous." But his real triumphs were still awaiting him at Lord & Thomas.

Hopkins was the first true advertising copywriter. He believed it was ineffective to say, in essence, "Buy my brand instead of the other fellow's." He felt advertising should say, "Let me show you why it is better for you to buy my brand." He used to say, "No argument can compete with one dramatic demonstration." Thus was "reason-why" advertising born.

Together with John E. Kennedy, Lasker and Hopkins constructed a concept of advertising that changed the nature of the craft, that has probably had a profound influence on our economy, and from which the whole business learned. Many early Lord & Thomas employees, having apprenticed with these two remarkable men, went on to start their own agencies. Among them were William Benton of Benton & Bowles, John Orr Young of Young & Rubicam, Charles Erwin and Louis Wasey of Erwin & Wasey, and Hill Blacket and Frank Hummert of Blacket, Sample & Hummert (now known as Dancer, Fitzgerald & Sample). Furthermore, the influence of Claude Hopkins is obvious in most books written about advertising in recent years, notably *Reality in Advertising* by Rosser Reeves and *Confessions of an Advertising Man* by David Ogilvy. The influence is graciously acknowledged in the latter. Mr. Ogilvy is a gracious gentleman.

JOHN O'TOOLE

In December 1942, Albert Lasker decided he had had enough
of the advertising business. Used to dealing directly with the
men who had built great enterprises, he had no stomach for the
trend toward pushing advertising responsibility down to juniors.
Additionally, he wanted to devote more time to his many other
interests. He decided the name Lord & Thomas was to retire
with him, but he sold the physical assets of the company to Fax,
Emerson Foote and Don Belding for $168,000 (today that might
buy you about 4,500 shares of the company's stock). He also
agreed to visit the clients and recommend that they stay with
the successor company, which, for phonetic reasons, would be
called Foote, Cone & Belding. All but two of them did.

Probably the most traumatic event in the early years of FCB,
and certainly the most highly publicized, was the agency's res-
ignation of the American Tobacco account in 1948. It was one
of the largest accounts in all of advertising. The budgets for
Lucky Strike and Pall Mall cigarettes came to $12,000,000—about
a fourth of the agency's total volume. It was resigned because, in
the words of Emerson Foote, "It is no longer possible to do the kind
of advertising for Lucky Strike that built the brand." The new
president of American Tobacco, Vincent Riggio, suffered from
such acute indecision and acted from such a limited understanding of advertising that planning was impossible and advertising
effectiveness diminished. Foote concluded that the agency could no
longer be proud of the work it did for this client. Cone and
Belding concurred.

Emerson Foote left the company due to illness in 1952. Don
Belding retired in 1959 and died before seeing the company
celebrate its hundredth year in 1973. But even before those
events, it was clear that Fairfax Cone was the successor to
Albert Lasker. The agency pulled out of the American Tobacco
trauma easily and, under Fax's leadership, grew into something
bigger and more diverse than even Lasker, who died in 1952,
could have imagined.

For someone who's serious about the craft, Foote, Cone &
Belding is a good place to develop the proper attitudes towards
it. In the tradition of the company, in the legacy of Lasker and

the insights of Hopkins, in the wisdom of Cone and the contributions of hundreds of other perceptive people, in this 108-year-old reservoir of experience and knowledge, is the key to what advertising is all about. At least, I found it there. And that is the primary reason I've stayed in advertising and in FCB for half my life.

Persons, not people

An understanding of what advertising is all about is essential for two reasons. Without it we can't create ads and commercials that produce the maximum results for an advertiser, that fully accomplish his objectives, that persuade as many prospects as possible to buy his product. In addition, without it we are certainly going to run afoul of the terms of the implicit contract; we are going to insult our prospects' intelligence or bore them or worse. I believe results and respect for consumers go hand in hand. Furthermore, I believe that divorcing the two produces unhappy consequences more frequently than is generally recognized.

The trouble lies not in advertising, which in itself and of its basic nature is benign. The trouble lies in the attitudes some practitioners bring to it—attitudes resulting from a failure to comprehend what it's all about.

And what it's all about is persons. Not people, but persons. If advertising is essentially salesmanship, this has to be true. An effective salesman learns as much as he can about his prospect before making his call, tries to fit his approach to his best estimation of that individual's personal needs and way of life. He doesn't rattle off a canned pitch to every prospect or to large groups of both prospects and nonprospects.

And yet a good deal of advertising does just that. Part of the problem originates in the kind of information on which advertising planning is based—and in the attitudes that will accept it as adequate. For example, it is traditional for the research department in an agency to provide a description of the "target market" to the creative department as work commences. This is

84

usually put in "demographic" terms and sounds pretty much like this:

> Our target is a housewife or working woman, 18 to
> 49 years old, minimum household income of $20,000
> per year, some college education, primarily urban,
> white, married or divorced.

It sounds sufficiently definitive until you start thinking about it. Then you realize that while it's a description of Phyllis Schlafly, ardent campaigner for traditional women's roles and against the Equal Rights Amendment, it's also a description of Gloria Steinem. Within those demographic walls live Anita Bryant and Jane Fonda. Even Renee Richards.

Most responses to an ad or commercial are neutral. In the split second when the initial evaluation is made, most persons conclude, "It's not for me." They turn the page or turn off their minds. If they aren't prospects, little is lost. It's all right with me if a nonsmoker slips past a Kent ad or if a man stops watching a Miss Clairol commercial.

In other cases, a person's response to an advertisement is instantly positive. If he were to articulate it, it would be, "Hey, they're talking to *me*. They're saying something important to me." A personal, one-to-one relationship is established. And when that happens, as it does millions of times a day, something beautiful ensues for both parties.

But in a few cases, the response will be negative. The individual will perceive that the message is intended for him but find that it bores him or insults his intelligence or even offends or enrages him.

The difference lies in whether the message is based on a knowledge of—and is directed to—*people* or a *person*. Although they fit the same demographic profile, it is difficult for me to believe that Anita Bryant and Jane Fonda could perceive certain messages for certain products in similar ways. They are the same *people* but very different *persons*.

Advertising that ignores those differences, that talks to either woman in terms of the other's values in hopes of reaching both, can never elicit the response "Hey, they're talking to *me*." But advertising that speaks personally to each in her own terms, or bases its appeal on a shared emotional current that runs deeper than life-style differences, is far more likely to evoke that response, thus succeeding in its particular objectives and at the same time contributing to public attitudes that make all advertising more productive.

This is what makes advertising so frustrating and so exciting. It must make a specific statement to an individual, yet it rides on the coattails of mass communication media: networks and stations, magazines and newspapers, many of which are attempting to attract as many people as possible. At the same time, those people are increasingly demonstrating their diversity, their uniqueness, their identity as persons.

In historical terms, this latter development is relatively new. For generations, the "melting pot" idea dominated our thinking. The massive effort and common cause of World War II made us see ourselves as truly "one nation, under God" and "we, the people." Such concepts, conflicting more and more with reality, prevailed throughout the 1950s, aided by the most influential mass medium ever conceived, network television. Society became increasingly depersonalized. As the population grew, half of us jammed ourselves into less than one percent of the land mass. Computers came along to reduce us to numbers rather than names. The term "identity crisis" was coined. We found ourselves more and more part of a crowd.

Inevitably, in the 1960s, a revolution began to erupt—a rejection of "massism," conformism and faceless institutionalism. The Revolution of the Individual was upon us. We began dressing differently and growing our hair and expressing ourselves through nonwork activities. We began forming liberation groups: black, feminist, gay, consumer, anything. We began sounding off.

We also began saying something in our responses to mass communication. Television viewing started to drop off among the generation that had grown up with the tube. Mass circulation magazines began to have serious problems, and one by one, they all died. But meanwhile, special-interest and life-style publications like *Sports Illustrated, Sunset, Playboy, New York* and *TV Guide* flourished.

What Americans were saying was simply this: "I'm not part of a crowd, I'm a person. Pay some attention to me and what I need. Or else." They were saying it to governments, to industries, to advertising. Some advertising didn't listen. It continued to look at people in terms of demographics rather than as individuals united by common attitudes or life styles or perceptions of themselves. It continued to discount their intelligence in favor of some vast common denominator. It continued to shout at a crowd rather than talk to persons.

Sometimes this Pavlovian approach produced sales, but at the expense of the credibility and acceptance that provide the soil in which advertising flourishes. It was a kind of strip-mining for which we're paying a price now in negative public attitudes. But such offenses, while obviously memorable, were relatively rare in the enormous volume of advertising messages delivered daily. The better advertising agencies paid attention to what consumers were saying and even developed techniques to help themselves listen better.

George Gallup once told me that market research really began in the 1920s when Lord & Thomas was handling a canned evaporated milk account. The product was introduced in a test market in Indiana where the sell-in to retail stores was successful and displays of the product were in evidence everywhere as the advertising was launched. Sales were excellent in the initial weeks, then dropped to almost nothing. Obviously something about the product was discouraging repurchase. Lasker dispatched a goodly proportion of his staff to that Indiana town to knock on doors, talk to housewives and find out what it was (it turned out to be a slight almond taste that was easily corrected). And so another industry was born.

But the real turning point came when Lasker arrived at a conclusion that, though not surprising to at least some of us today, must have raised eyebrows if not hackles in the luncheon clubs of New York and Chicago in the twenties. He asserted that

the advertising agency is not really the representative of the manufacturer to the consumer but vice versa (more on this later).

Claude Hopkins consistently pointed out the need to know,
understand and write to a single, prototypical prospect. For
example: "When you plan and prepare an advertisement, keep
before you a typical buyer. Your subject, your headline has
gained his or her attention. Then, in everything, be guided by
what you would do if you met the buyer face-to-face. . . . Don't
think of people in the mass. That gives you a blurred view.
Think of a typical individual, man or woman, who is likely to
want what you sell." The specific and personal effect to be
sought, he once wrote, was "the impact of a bellboy calling a
man's name in a crowded room."

Fax Cone had maiden aunt Sarah, an elderly lady who lived
in California, voted the Socialist party ticket and was anti-business,
anti-advertising and anti-establishment in every way. On particularly tough assignments, where credibility was the key issue,
he would summon up a vision of Aunt Sarah and imagine
himself saying what he had written directly to her. If the vision
laughed in his face and turned away, he'd start again. A few
times he actually called her on the phone and tried headlines out
on her. The critical test was whether or not she'd hang up on
him.

Fax said he had turned to Aunt Sarah after his first copy chief
at Lord & Thomas, Walter Doty, left to edit *Sunset* magazine and
lead it to a position of eminence among American periodicals.
Doty used to drill this lesson into the brains of his writers:
"Write to one person. Aim what you have to say at someone who
has every reason to be interested. If the message is clear, then
everyone else who has any reason to be interested will get it too."
Fax passed the same message on to those of us who followed,
repeating it and rephrasing it over the years. In one memo I've
kept, he put it this way: "Let us make every advertisement that
we make *personal*. Let us aim it at *one* person, just as we
would in face-to-face contact."

I was hired at FCB by a feisty, brilliant and kind man named
Aloysius J. Bremner. Al headed the creative department in

Chicago from some point so deep in the past that I never inquired, right up to his retirement in 1968. I had the honor and the formidable challenge of taking his place. Al used to demand of his copywriters that they truly understand the prospect for each product. "Talk to him in a way that gets him nodding in agreement before you try to sell him something," he said again and again.

This personal approach to the planning and creation of advertising has characterized the method of all our best creative people. Shirley Polykoff was the copywriter who helped launch and build the hair-coloring industry with such Clairol campaigns as "Does She or Doesn't She?" and "Is It True Blondes Have More Fun?" Describing copywriting in her book entitled, not surprisingly, *Does She or Doesn't She?*, Shirley wrote, "It's rarely about products to a consumer. It's more a direct conversation *with* the consumer about a product."

Talking sympathetically, honestly, openly to the specific individual who was a prospect for Hallmark cards or Sunkist oranges, recognizing where the product would fit meaningfully into that person's life and which among its many features would be recognized as a welcome benefit, helped build those businesses. It boils down to the difference between "Aren't you glad you use Dial? Don't you wish everybody did?" and "Dial prevents B.O." Or the difference between "You're not getting older, you're getting better" and "Look years younger with Clairol's Loving Care."

With few exceptions, books on how to write advertising copy will tell you to immerse yourself in the product, study and restudy it, learn it inside and out. But most products just aren't that complex. They can be understood pretty clearly after a few days of intense concentration. As Lasker wrote, "After thousands of experiences, the advertising man comes instinctively to know the real selling point in a commodity or proposition. If he becomes too technical—which he is almost certain to do unless he has the viewpoint of the person he's trying to sell—he loses the greatest of talents." In reality, advertising is not about products but about a person and his life—and how the products can fit into that life to make it easier, richer or more rewarding.

It is the prospect who is difficult to define and understand, not the product. It is a study of the product in relation to your hard-won understanding of the prospect that is truly productive. This is what paves the way for the flash of insight that brings the two together personally, specifically and credibly. It is what produces advertising that gets into someone's heart rather than under his skin, advertising that makes friends as well as sales, advertising that works.

One Person to Another

There's a story, probably apocryphal, that's been kicking around the corridors of advertising agencies for three decades. Back in the pre-television era, it's said, an agency made a radio buy that seemed so right for the client, a regional coffee company, that the management supervisor himself went running over to tell the president of the client company about it. Escorted into the richly paneled office of the elderly and vastly successful chief executive, the adman described the one-hour Sunday afternoon program. Such was the prestige of the show that eight other sponsors had been vying for it. Yet the agency had managed to sign it, and for a reasonable price.

The client stared at him for a moment, then said, "Nobody will listen to it." The stricken adman mumbled, "But . . . but what makes you say that?" "Because on Sunday afternoon," replied the client, "everyone's out playing polo."

I wish I could say that attitude never really existed. And I wish I could say no one thinks like that today. But when I see commercials based on slick in-group jokes, when I hear dialogue delivered totally in New York-ese, when I see men depicted in commercials as either fat slobs or aged preppies and women reduced to nothing more than floor-scrubbing machinery, I can't escape the conclusion that some advertising people are still afflicted with terminal insularity.

THE TROUBLE WITH ADVERTISING . . .

All of my experience tells me that the advertising person who studies people as they really are, who is fascinated with what makes them do the things they do, who opens himself up to the rich and diverse society around him and applies what he learns there to his craft—that this person is the most successful. As I said earlier, the best creative people I know have always been amateur social psychologists. Some of them read every book that comes out on the subject. All of them try constantly to learn about people who live lives far different from their own, and some restless inner computer is always sorting out that information and relating it to advertising.

Though there are people in this business who, because of insecurity, harbor a disdain for anyone unknown to them, anyone unlike them, they don't last. To create effective advertising, writers and art directors must project themselves into the life, the mind, the heart of the person who is a prospect for their product. They must be able to virtually "become" that person. And to do that with consistency in an ever-changing society, they need help.

When I came to New York in 1969, I was struck by a number of phenomena, not the least strange of which was that advertising people seemed to travel in herds. It may be because the advertising business in New York is so big and important relative to its position in other cities in which I've worked. Whatever the cause, New York–based advertising people tend to lunch, dine, commute, drink, attend PTA meetings and, in some cases, live together to a degree unparalleled in my experience elsewhere. While we are, I must admit, thoroughly fascinating people, the result of intellectual incest is similar to that of the physical variety: idiots.

In a small attempt to ameliorate this insularity, I inaugurated a monthly luncheon in FCB offices where we would invite someone from whom we could learn about communication through means other than advertising. The idea was to have no more than eight of us around the luncheon table so as to encourage conversation rather than speeches and to learn something about

91

people from those who had been successful in affecting them in large numbers.

Since I had just read an article by Robert Montgomery in which he excoriated advertising and advertising people, I thought I'd start with him. As an eminently successful actor, director and producer, he certainly qualified as a communicator from whom we could learn. So I picked up the phone and called him. He was, I think, so relieved that I wasn't calling to attack his article that he accepted the invitation.

It turned out to be a delightful and productive hour and a half. We talked about his days as a producer of television drama, a career he was giving up with no little disillusionment about clients and agencies. We talked about his perceptions of who his audience was and how he was trying to affect them in several of his films, including the experimental, objective-camera feature *Lady in the Lake*, which he directed as well as played in. We learned something that day. I like to think Robert Montgomery did, too. Something about advertising people.

We've continued this very pleasant technique of learning about people—secondhand, so to speak—right up to this writing. We've had several other people from the stage, among them Alexis Smith and Ethel Merman. Trying to learn from dancers about communicating to an audience without words, we had lively conversations with Melissa Hayden, the great ballerina of Balanchine's New York City Ballet Company, and Donna McKechnie, the star of *A Chorus Line*.

In an attempt to understand the prototypical individual an editor has in mind as he or she accepts, rejects and alters material, we have lunched with the editors of the *New York Times*, the *Village Voice*, the *New York Post*, the *New Yorker*, *New York*, *Cosmopolitan*, *Esquire*, *Scientific American*, *Forbes*, *Ms.*, *Ladies' Home Journal*, the *Wall Street Journal* and *Newsweek*. Seeking a similar understanding of how the television journalist sees and writes to his viewer, we have talked with Elmer Lower, Jim McKay, Howard Cosell, Barbara Walters and Harry Reasoner of ABC; Walter Cronkite and Mike Wallace of CBS; Hugh Downs,

Edwin Newman and the late Frank McGee of NBC; and Bill Moyers of the Public Broadcasting Corporation.

We've talked with Bess Myerson about consumerism, LeRoy Neiman about painting, David Susskind about drama, Schuyler Chapin about opera, Eugene McCarthy about politics and George Gallup about people in general. And, of course, I've invited poets. We had an animated discussion with James Dickey and a memorable visit with W. H. Auden shortly before his return to England and his death in 1973.

Obviously there is as much enjoyment as elucidation in these luncheons. I do it because I like to. But I am convinced that I and the others attending have learned much of value about the consumers we're talking to on behalf of our clients from those who address them so successfully on behalf of other interests.

But to the practicing advertising person, to the professional who realizes his obligation to stay tuned in to people, the real feelings and thoughts of consumers themselves are far more useful than such secondhand knowledge. Getting at them is hard but essential work. At our agency we subscribe to and make required reading of public opinion polls published by the Roper Research Center or taken from the Yankelovich studies of social value trends and from Leo Shapiro's reports on the economic mood of the society.

And we have some other ways to get in closer touch with individual consumers and avoid the "ivory tower" syndrome that seems endemic to people in advertising agencies. One is personal contact with consumers. Every one of our operations around the world conducts, on a regular basis, discussion sessions with consumer groups, usually led by a trained researcher. Even more productive are consumer workshops that bring a small number of agency people and consumers together for a group discussion. It begins with a conversation about the lives the consumers lead, then swings quickly into how they perceive the product category and our product, how they use it, what they see as the real benefits. We pay close attention to the actual words they use.

Another kind of dialogue is achieved by telephone surveys.

JOHN O'TOOLE

There's nothing unusual about doing consumer surveys by phone, but the twist here is that the interviewing is done by agency people, not by professional pollsters, because the primary purpose is to understand consumers. What's the difference? It's the difference between reading in a research report that "24% of respondents indicated moderate to high dissatisfaction with the flavor characteristics of the product" and hearing a lady in West Covina tell you, "My kids say it tastes like soap. I'll never buy that crap again."

In both consumer workshops and telephone surveys, the questions have to do with specific products, social trends or consumer needs. And the information they yield, while not always representing a large or varied enough sample to project from, is invaluable for the insights it provides and the feeling it gives for a consumer's intensity, or lack of intensity, about a specific subject.

If a particular insight seems so important that we want to know if it holds true beyond one geographical area, we plug questions into the ongoing program of a large consumer research company, which allows us to ask questions of their national probability sample of 1,500 men and women. In addition, we send our people out to work in retail stores (one copywriter tended bar for a week in a Milwaukee tavern). We accompany shoppers as they go through a supermarket making decisions at the point of purchase. The purpose of all these activities is simply to know the consumer.

The real benefit of this approach is a more specifically appealing, more personally involving kind of advertising. But it has also produced a few gold nuggets for us. In 1976 Lorillard launched Kent Golden Lights, a low-tar-and-nicotine cigarette, now known simply as Golden Lights. It rapidly became a substantial new brand, a rare accomplishment since cigarettes withdrew from broadcast media. A number of other low-tar brands came on the market in 1976, but the advertising for Kent Golden Lights differed from that of the rest in one important respect. And that difference is largely attributable to the knowledge and understanding gained in a consumer workshop.

94

Conventional research clearly showed that certain smokers were concerned about tar content and would switch to a brand lower in tar than their own if they were assured of good taste. This we could promise them and did with the headline "Kent Golden Lights at 8 mgs. tar. As low as you can go and still get good taste." With a powerful competitor from Philip Morris at 9 mgs. tar (Merit) and some new entries at 2 mgs., this seemed to be a promising position.

During the course of creative development, we brought scores of cigarette smokers into our "living room" to talk about their lives, their cigarettes, their perceptions of other brands and their feelings about tar content. And we began to notice something. While all indicated interest in a low-tar brand, and while 8 mgs. sounded low to them, hardly anyone knew the tar content of his own brand. We got on the telephone and began chatting with more people. When we had a dialogue going, we asked each to tell us the tar content of his or her brand. Practically no one knew.

It was obvious that our headline could only be effective if we provided the knowledge that would make 8 mgs. important: the tar content of a prospect's own brand. That's why, unlike the advertising for other low-tar products, ads for Kent Golden Lights featured a number of competitive packages. A smoker's eye went right to his own brand—or, as one man said, "It's like when you see your high school class photograph. You immediately start looking for yourself." Under his brand he found its tar content. Then "8 mgs. tar" became an important difference.

In another case, a copywriter for Hallmark was interviewing a woman who, in the course of the conversation, mentioned that she kept all the greeting cards she received over the years and now and then went through them to relive memories. Here was an advantage we hadn't considered: the longevity of a greeting card as opposed to a phone call or flowers. Soon the information from that conversation became a beautiful two-minute commercial for *The Hallmark Hall of Fame*, one that provided yet another reason for buying a Hallmark card.

Insights like these, which can only be gleaned from a close

association with the real prospect for a product, can be worth millions of dollars in sales to our clients. And the attitude that motivates a search for them, the drive to know and understand the prospect thoroughly and sympathetically, the resolve to present the product and its benefits in terms of the reality of the prospect's unique life—this is what advertising is all about.

The kind of advertising that produces results today and a fertile ground for advertising tomorrow is that which most closely approximates one human being talking with another.

The Nod of Agreement

It's difficult to damage the implicit contract too egregiously—or to make many other mistakes in advertising—if you keep in mind the analogy to a personal sales call, particularly when considering the opening: the first element the prospect's eye will perceive on the page or the first statement that will be made to the eye and/or ear on the screen.

Certain conclusions seem irrefutable. If you walked into someone's home shouting, as some announcers and headlines do, it's not likely that the resident would take kindly to the substance of your message. If, first off, you pushed an ugly picture under his nose, he probably wouldn't stay put long enough to hear you explain that it's not a picture of what you're selling but of what you're proposing to cure. If you open with a statement that bores him, that has nothing to do with his interests or that simply bewilders him, there's no reason to assume he's going to listen further.

When executing advertising, it's best to think of yourself as an uninvited guest in the living room of a prospect who has the magical power to make you disappear instantly. Because that is the situation an ad, even a commercial, really encounters. This is not to say that we're trying to dupe people into believing that we're there for any purpose other than to sell something. Consumers are not idiots. They can tell an ad from an editorial, a commercial from a program. And they know what selling is all about. Millennia of trading and bartering and marketing have not left us totally innocent. It's how the advertisement approaches the prospect that makes most of the difference. The first few seconds of looking, reading or listening determine whether the prospect will open himself to what you are saying or withdraw into a mental carapace.

The best advice I ever received on this subject was that remark by Al Bremner. I first heard it while struggling with a headline for the Sunbeam Shavemaster, an electric shaver distinguished by the fact that it had three long blades sweeping back and forth under the head rather than operating on the traditional "clipper" principle. I forget what tortuous statement I composed about the product's superiority. I'm sure it wasn't good enough to get a blade-and-lather man to respond with anything but an amused grunt. But Al pulled five simple words from somewhere in my body copy and said, "Now, there's something that guy will nod in agreement with." The line was: "Nothing shaves like a blade."

The same principle underlies just about all the best headlines that have come out of FCB, from the classic "Don't put a cold in your pocket" for Kleenex tissues to "If I've only one life, let me live it as a blonde" for Lady Clairol hair color. The attendant pitfall is best demonstrated by an exaggerated but authentic example I saw many years ago in a newspaper ad: "Lincoln was a great president. Lincoln Savings is a great bank." You're nodding in agreement with the first statement even as you're falling into the gaping *non sequitur*. What elicits the nod must obviously have something to do with the prospect's life, something to do with the product, and something to do with how the two come together to form a benefit.

And the key word is *benefit*. It is not a product feature but the benefit a product brings to an individual's life that turns the nod of agreement into the spark of interest. A product feature is the product seen through the eyes of the manufacturer. The benefit is the product seen through the eyes of a consumer. The difference is critical. Albert Lasker wrote, "The advertising agent really does not represent the manufacturer. He represents the public to the manufacturer and, in turn, is the manufacturer's representative to the public." Or, as Shirley Polykoff often put it, "I'm just an articulate consumer in the client's offices."

In this role, the most important function we perform is to divert the client's understandable fascination with the features he built into the product and make him look at it in terms of the consumer's equally understandable question "What's in it for me?" For example, the Sunbeam Shavemaster I mentioned could have been presented as "the only shaver with three stainless steel blades sweeping back and forth under a thin curved head." But what's in it for me? Very little if that statement isn't preceded by something that suggests a benefit: a shave like the one I'm used to getting from a blade.

A lot of interesting things could be said about the technological advances that permitted thinner walls in an automotive battery, thereby increasing the volume of water, acid and plate surface. Instead, the commercials made a benefit statement: "The DieHard. Starts your car when most other batteries won't." And the statement was preceded by a demonstration that had the prospect nodding in agreement. Similarly, there are dozens of unique product features in International Harvester's Rotary Cultivators. But our headline, the element that got the farmer nodding in agreement, went right to the benefit: "Clean up your middles. Condition your soil. Mulch your beds. All at 14 acres per hour." What farmer is going to shake his head at that?

The statements that are most successful in getting heads nodding in agreement—and that are somehow the most difficult to bring off—are those that smack so clearly of honesty and candor that they disarm the prospect and dilute his natural inclination to distrust. It might be the confident, factual wording, as in the International Harvester ad cited above. It might be the way in which the statement recognizes the mental set of the prospect, as in a multi-picture service ad with the headline "More, perhaps, than you care to know about Sunkist Lemons." Or it might be the open admission of a seeming negative, as in the great Doyle

Dane Bernbach campaign for Avis: "We're #2. So we try harder." You can almost see those heads nodding.

At the risk of sounding insipid, I might add that another way to achieve a successful opening statement is to be nice. Remember that analogy about our being an uninvited guest in the living room of someone with the power to make us disappear. If you were representing a steel company, would you open with this statement from an ad Fax Cone once used to demonstrate the point: "How would you like an acid bath?" The response is likely to be "How would you like a punch in the mouth?" Or, if you were trying to interest your prospect in a new solid antiperspirant, would you start with "Get off the can. Get on the stick"? One national advertiser did. Anyone who answers either of those questions with a yes doesn't yet understand what advertising is all about. On the other hand, "Aren't you glad you use Dial Soap? Don't you wish everyone did?" opens a rather delicate subject in a way that's nice. And, the results would suggest, extremely effective.

It's not nice to assume that prospects are looking for the cheapest item in any category rather than the best value for themselves or their families. The secret of Kraft Dinners advertising is the visual, an appetizing photograph of good food in a quality setting, *in combination* with headlines such as "How to make ends meet" and "Only pennies per serving." The secret behind the Sears national television sales is a demonstration of product quality followed by the announcement of a specially reduced price.

It's not nice to insult people's intelligence. Tossing the competitor's product into a garbage can isn't going to ingratiate us with someone who has thoughtfully chosen that brand. A liquor advertiser once showed a bottle of Beefeater gin knocked over on its side in order to put his bottle in a better light. This opens no dialogue with me if I've recently paid the price necessary to acquire a quart of Beefeater. My defenses are up. He's implied I'm a patsy. And it's going to take more logic and persuasion than he has in his bag to bring me around.

There's an element of implied insult in some comparative

advertising that's being done today. Forcing a comparison be-tween a relatively unknown product and the category leader, or between an inexpensive entry and the most costly, simply because they share one or two superficial features fools no one. But in trying, you've demonstrated your low opinion of consumers' good sense. And since most people think of themselves as pretty smart shoppers, they sit through your message—if they stay with you at all—closed to persuasion rather than nodding in agreement.

It's not difficult to elicit the nod of agreement if we truly know and understand the individuals we're approaching, if we've examined the product and the category through their eyes and from the viewpoint of their lives, and if we start talking to them in a personal, human way. Then we might open the dialogue with an insight the two of us share. If we're addressing a woman who has just spotted those first gray hairs and is beset by the worries such an experience brings in a youth-enamored society, we might say, "You're not getting older. You're getting better." Or, if we're talking to a twelve- or thirteen-year-old girl about Kotex, we might begin with "Dear Mother Nature: drop dead."

In dealing with a mass audience on behalf of a product whose appeal is so broad that the advertising cannot be focused on any particular attitudinal or life-style group, the best way to get heads nodding in agreement is to find a level that transcends individual differences, to demonstrate that we and our prospect share some emotional current of universal resonance. An ad for a simple product like Kraft Jet-Puffed Marshmallows did this when it showed an engaging little boy holding a big bag of marshmallows and then said, "A marshmallow a day makes your blue eyes bluer."

A commercial for Hallmark cards did it when it depicted the less than satisfying day of an office worker, from missing the bus in the morning to getting caught without her umbrella in an evening shower, right up to the moment she opened her mail and discovered that someone had thought about her with a Hallmark card. A commercial for Sunkist oranges did it when a little girl, the daughter of the Sunkist grower who was narrating the product story, held a fresh-picked orange for the camera but was unable to control a self-conscious giggle.

Another for Sears Hug-along Hosiery did it by demonstrating that since women come in different sizes, so should pantyhose. Compelled to announce her height and weight, the most ample of the four girls in the commercial quickly added, "I've got big bones." And a spot for Idaho potatoes did it when the narrator, Cecil Andrus, at the time governor of Idaho, showed us how he prepared his own dinner when his wife was away. He was wearing his wife's apron. And he was doing no better at it than I would.

Some of these examples begin to raise the question of humor in advertising. Humor is an emotional response like love, anger, nostalgia, frustration, pride in achievement, and grief. Unlike them, however, it can be intellectualized to distinguish an "in-group" from an "out-group." That's what "camp" humor is all about, and that's why it will close up more prospects than it will reach when used in advertising.

Moreover, humor, being the complex social phenomenon it is—a catharsis, a release from tension—is often based on putting someone down, inflicting humiliation. The pie-in-the-face and the pratfall may be legitimate devices of show business, but in advertising they are going to get more people shaking their heads than nodding, more prospects sympathizing with the recipient of the pie than with the deliverer.

The kind of humor to employ in advertising is the kind that demonstrates an insight into the human condition, one the advertiser shares with the prospect. It's the kind of situation exemplified by a Sears Forecast Luggage commercial in which everybody abuses the poor guy's new suitcase, from the cab driver who casually heaves it into his trunk to the airline baggage attendant who drops it with a thud onto the ramp. The man's reaction lets us share a smile at the injustice of things rather than making us guffaw at some poor boob's plight. It is the former that gets heads nodding in agreement.

JOHN O'TOOLE

The Maker's Mark

Off and on, for as long as I can recall, McGraw-Hill Magazines
has run an ad in the trade publications of our business that
pictures a stern, if not hostile, gent fixing you with a cold stare
from his desk chair. He's saying, "I don't know who you are. I
don't know your company. I don't know your company's product. I don't know what your company stands for. I don't know
your company's customers. I don't know your company's record. I don't know your company's reputation. Now—what was
it you wanted to sell me?"

McGraw-Hill develops from that a good case for advertising
in industry magazines. I find it an excellent reminder of the
necessity of making the personality, the identity of the advertiser an important and continuing part of his advertising. A
recognition of this necessity demonstrates, in an advertising
person, another attitude essential to effective advertisements and
to the longevity of the implicit contract. For if advertising works
best when it approximates a person-to-person dialogue, there
must be some unique, recognizable and personal entity opening
the conversation with the prospect. The present state of society
makes this consideration more essential than ever, but it has
always been an important element in effective advertising. Claude
Hopkins said back in 1923, "We try to give each advertiser a
becoming style. We make him distinctive, perhaps not in appearance, but in manner and tone."

In 1976 I went to South Africa, where national television
had just become a reality. I had been asked to conduct a seminar
on television advertising based essentially on our experience in
the United States. As part of it, I put together a reel of six Dial
soap commercials representing campaigns from 1951 to 1976. The
overall impression of continuity was astonishing, despite dramatic changes in color, cinematography, editing, clothing, models and even modes of speech over twenty-five years. Dial

clearly had an identity that constantly adapted to the times but never fundamentally changed.

Later that year I tried something similar for a meeting of all our managers from around the world. I chose one successful product from each of our areas in the United States: Clairol's Loving Care from New York, Sunkist oranges from Los Angeles and, again, Dial soap from Chicago. This time I went back just ten years but showed six to eight commercials plus the magazine advertising for each brand. Once again the effect was undeniable. Over a decade that had seen competitive brands flitting from one identity to the next, these products exhibited recognizable and continuing personalities, even though the commercials had gone through many executional variations, a number of ideas and in two cases strategy changes.

More recently we did a similar demonstration for the island of Bermuda. We looked at examples of magazine ads we had done for them since being assigned in 1973. The identity was strong and consistent. Then we took a similar look at the campaigns of competitive vacation destinations. The identities varied widely and frequently.

What a tremendous asset a clear identity is for an advertiser. It is a substitute for the personal presence that was first an essential part of the relationship between maker and buyer and later obtained in the interaction between the maker's salesman and the buyer. It compensates for the fact that there is no longer a grocer at the grocery store or a druggist at the drugstore to tell consumers about the products for sale there. It's the surrogate presence of the manufacturer.

But if that's what it is, there are a number of things it is not. It is not the personal style of a copywriter or art director. On the contrary, creative people must be able to identify the advertiser's uniqueness and slip into it, work from it. As Hopkins said, "Before a man writes a new ad on that line, he gets into the spirit adopted by the advertiser. He plays a part as an actor plays it." It is also not the image an agency wants to project for itself superimposed on every ad for every client. Nor is it "brand image."

During the fifties and sixties, it was popular to work out a personality, or "image," for each brand to set it apart from the competition. Companies developed these personalities brand by brand, with little thought to any relationship among them. The motivation was simply to present a different face among those already present in the category. Once a useful tool, brand-image thinking just isn't up to the job today.

How many salesmen could you remember if you spent a day interviewing 475 of them? Yet 475 is the number of messages that appeared on Channel 2, New York, one day when we happened to be counting. The result, as several recent studies seem to indicate, is a growing inability on the part of the viewer to identify the brand by means of its brand image. As for magazines, the December 1980 issue of *McCall's* carried 183 individual ads. At the very least, you have to ask, "Is there a maximum number of brand images the human mind can retain? Even if it wants to?"

Moreover, a brand image has to be consistent to be effective. As campaigns change, you have to be a real devotee of advertising to keep up with what a lot of products are purporting to be. And few, even those interested enough to be reading this book, could be described as devotees of advertising. There is nothing more wasteful in advertising than constant and arbitrary changes of campaign for a product, yearly wrenches in the product's promise to its prospect, dictated by a slightly better "score" in testing or just by a desire for "something fresh." Advertising takes time to get up speed, especially for infrequently purchased products. Continuity adds to the effect of each new message in a campaign. For most products, one good campaign over a five-year period is better than five very good campaigns over the same span.

Changing market conditions will of course necessitate strategy shifts from time to time, just as societal changes will require executional variations. What I'm talking about goes beyond strategy, idea and execution but is always present in all three. It goes beyond the image of a company's individual brands but is reflected in each of them. It is the character of the company—or, more accurately, of the persons who today represent the continuity of the company and who stand behind its products or provide its services.

Every advertiser company I've ever worked for has had some quality that made it unique: its attitude about itself, its customers, its competition, its future, its past; how it feels about the products it makes; how it views its obligations to people who use those products; its concerns about the industry, the society, the environment, the nation, the world. Recently several business writers have begun to notice this phenomenon and refer to it as a "corporate culture."

The distillation of these qualities into a frame of mind about the client—one that consistently influences the choice of graphics, type, language, announcer, color, music, in a discernible way over a long period of time—is what I call establishing the maker's mark. Cumulatively and inevitably this process defines an identity—nonverbal perhaps, but real and unique—that people can recognize and respond to in that marketer's advertising for all its products. Or, if it's a one-product company, it provides a basis for acceptance as the product is extended into other lines. Capturing it requires an immersion in the company, its philosophies, its functions, large and small, its people and in particular its leader.

The unique identity is probably most apparent in those companies still run by the founding genius. During the 1960s we worked for Sara Lee, a bakery that made, froze and distributed nationally some of the most delectable pastry products I've ever encountered this side of a fine restaurant or a specialty baked goods shop. At the time the company was still led by the baker who had founded it on the North Side of Chicago and proudly named it after his only daughter. His name was Charlie Lubin, a jolly man with glasses like the bottoms of bottles and a tummy that bespoke his devotion to the craft.

Charlie represented to all his associates an obsession with quality. As I got to know him, he represented the identity that I, as the creative director, had to synthesize in the advertising for his product. For example, the first time I went through the plant, a

105

meticulously clean facility not far from his original bakery, I saw a group of women unwrapping packages of Kraft's Philadelphia Brand cream cheese. When I asked about this, I found that it went on all day every day. Charlie's palate told him that Kraft was the best cream cheese made, and only the best could go into his cheesecake. The fact that Kraft would not sell it to him in bulk didn't deter him.

I remember asking him about the butter he used in his Danish pastry. The best-quality butter I could find in a grocery store was 92 score; Sara Lee used 93 score. I asked Charlie if he thought even the most discriminating customer could tell the difference. "Naw," he said. "But let me tell you something." He turned and pointed to the area where the other officers of the company sat, the colleagues with whom he daily engaged in violent shouting matches that passed, at Sara Lee, for business discussions. "See those guys out there? They're just waiting for me to say, 'Okay, let's buy 92 score butter.' Then they'll start pushing me to go with powdered eggs, dry milk, second-grade fruit. I don't care if nobody can taste the difference. We're sticking with 93 score."

Charlie Lubin's fierce devotion to quality for the sake of quality was the heart of the maker's mark. I worked to infuse it into the advertising for his many magnificent products. (Perhaps it's something in the Lake Michigan water, but Charlie, like Mayor Daley, was given to malapropisms. I remember him telling me that the best advertising was "mouth-to-mouth advertising.") The TV commercials showed the glorious ingredients, the baking and the mouth-watering results while the sound track let us listen in on a couple, perhaps watching TV in bed, commenting on what they were seeing until temptation drove them out to the kitchen to unfreeze a Sara Lee goodie for themselves.

Charlie sold Sara Lee to Consolidated Foods and several years later retired. The new manager thought little of the old maker's mark or, for that matter, the old agency. We were fired. The new agency abandoned our campaign, and expressions of quality gave way to empty wordplay: "Everybody doesn't like something, but nobody doesn't like Sara Lee." That was 1967. The campaign and the agency were replaced. So was the manager. In 1981 Sara Lee came home again to Foote, Cone & Belding.

The founder is not the sole key to a company's identity, which is fortunate since he might not be available for interviewing. In at least three companies we work for, the descendants of the founder are running the businesses with vigor, are articulate spokesmen for their unique traits and standards, and see to the preservation of these things with diligence.

Joyce C. Hall, the founder of Hallmark Cards, is now retired. But his son, Donald, continues the company's course of growth and its dedication to taste as a sort of eighties version of his amazing father. Sam Johnson, great-grandson of the founder of Johnson's Wax, is much the same kind of leader, concerned about maintaining the product quality and social responsibility that are implicit in that corporate name. And the gracious and elegant José Ignacio Domecq today guides the company in Jerez, Spain, that was founded by his ancestors over two centuries ago and has been producing some of the world's finest sherries and brandies ever since. He is the final authority on whether or not the contents of a particular cask are excellent enough to bear the name Pedro Domecq.

These are proud and committed men. Each can provide you with the elements of his company's maker's mark. Each will do so with enthusiasm. But so can others who lead nonfamily businesses of no little importance and character. Lorillard is America's oldest tobacco company, rich in lore. And its president, Curt Judge, has profound respect for that heritage and the responsibilities that go with it. The same is true of Dave Duensing, chairman of Armour-Dial, the company formed out of a Chicago meat packer's successful sortie against the three giant soap manufacturers. These companies are owned today by larger corporations that realize the value of the identities they have acquired and would do nothing to vitiate them. Nor would the current presidents allow it to happen.

In addition to the leader, there are generally others around the company whose affection for and dedication to the enterprise help define its personality: the capable woman in accounting who's been there since high school graduation, the production foreman whom every competitor has unsuccessfully tried to hire away, the audiovisual man or inventory manager to whom everyone goes with questions no one else can answer. The secret to arriving at a company's unique identity is talking with, and listening to, all these people. As you do, you begin to get the clues, the differences. Those differences are often as distinct and meaningful as the features built into the product. And they are the stuff of which the maker's mark is fashioned.

It doesn't come easily. It's often difficult for managements to agree on exactly what they stand for. Or to articulate it in anything but vague platitudes. Or to accept an objective view of their identity, positve as it might be, rather than a subjective view of what they'd rather be. Furthermore, when this ephemeral thing is finally captured, when it begins flavoring every piece of advertising, when it begins working and people begin to feel it, that's when someone will want to change it—even though it may be a more valuable asset than any appearing on the corporate books.

Abandoning that identity at the first competitive attack, or with the arrival of a new marketing director, is a tragedy. That's when it's essential that customers be able to relate to the people behind the product, particularly if the product promise is changed. To quote Hopkins again,

> In successful advertising, great pains are taken never to change our tone. That which won so many is probably the best way to win others. Then people come to know us. We build on that acquaintance rather than introduce a stranger in strange guise. People do not know us by name alone, but by looks and mannerisms. Appearing different every time we meet never builds up confidence.

This advice from the past has taken on new importance in recent years as companies have had to respond to criticism from government and special-interest groups in issue-oriented messages, or, as I dubbed it back in 1974, advocacy advertising. When you have to present your point of view, often unpopular, in the heat of raging controversy, what a boon it is to be able to do so from an identity base that's recognizable, familiar and positively regarded by consumers.

The elements of an advertiser's maker's mark can be conveyed by any or all of the communications tools available. Most often a verbal statement is part of it. "The quality goes in before the name goes on" begins to tell you something about the people who make Zenith products. And over decades, it becomes an assurance that those people strive to live up to the banner they've chosen to work under.

You begin to feel the personal presence of Hallmark from "When you care enough to send the very best"; of Kraft from "Good food and good food ideas"; of Dial soap from "Aren't you glad you use Dial? Don't you wish everybody did?" A product message suggests a further dimension of appeal by the simple addition of "New from Johnson's Wax." It's significant that in a national survey done in 1977 by R. H. Bruskin Associates, when 2,531 respondents were asked to rate eleven corporate slogans as completely true, partially true or untrue, Hallmark's line came out on top; 62% said it was completely true. In third place was Zenith's slogan.

But the maker's mark is not limited to words. Advertising for Bermuda, while characterized by a summation line and an unusual copy treatment, makes its strongest statement about the unique qualities of the island, its people and its visitors with its layout and graphic approach. A personality can also be part of the maker's mark: the governor of Idaho for that state's potatoes; a particular model, such as Lauren Hutton for Revlon; a spokesman like Robert Morley for British Airways; the disembodied voice of Ed Herlihy for Kraft. Anything that goes into the making of an ad or commercial can contribute to the maker's mark. The important thing is that all the elements add up to a communications expression of the unique reality of the advertiser, one that can provide a consistent background for strategic thinking, idea generation and creative execution.

For example, the distinctive identity in the advertising for Dial soap over a quarter of a century was apparent even to those audiences in South Africa who hadn't lived with the commercials as we have here. It has to do with people at Armour like Dave Duensing who made the original decisions on how the product would position and conduct itself, and who maintained this basic attitude despite massive onslaughts from Lifebuoy, Zest, Irish Spring and Safeguard. It's a stance rooted in the positive benefits a specific human being derives from using the product: confidence, refreshment, cleanliness. It's a refusal to concentrate on the negative ramifications of not using it. It's friendliness, it's helpfulness, it's respect.

Clairol's identity extends over a variety of hair-coloring and hair-care products for prospects ranging from teenagers to grandmothers. It stems from an attitude about women, an empathy with the importance a woman puts on her hair and the serious emotional commitment that goes with a decision to change it in any way.

Few advertisers place more value on their identity—or pay more attention to retaining their maker's mark in every advertisement—than Kraft. Implicit in each ad and commercial, directing its photography, propping, tone of voice and basic approach, is a promise of product quality and an understanding of what a housewife's job is and what can help her do that job more successfully and less expensively.

Kraft recognizes, too, that the media vehicles should also reflect their maker's mark, which is why they are intensely concerned with the content of the programs that carry their commercials. But no advertiser has made the medium as much a part of its maker's mark as has Hallmark. Each program selected and produced for *The Hallmark Hall of Fame* must be compatible with the essential identity expressed in the commercials: a group of tasteful and considerate people dedicated to the basic human attribute of thoughtfulness, whose every product is something you buy, not for yourself, but for someone else.

Levi Strauss has a vivid, clear-cut identity that is present as a maker's mark in all its consumer communications: young, irreverent, unpretentious, practical and imaginative. British Airways reflects British quality and dependability, all in the context of warmth and concern for people. Its identity is summed up in "We take more care of you." Sears, Roebuck and Co. is, in its advertising, just what it is in its stores: good old Sears. While the subject matter of the advertising ranges from diamonds to dresses to DieHard batteries, the underlying character of Sears is always there: demonstrable product quality and a darn good price—that's value.

Most companies have this kind of uniqueness about them, an appealing set of standards or beliefs or aspirations that can make their products more valuable, their advertising more memorable and their promises more believable. As Fax Cone said, "The fact of the matter is that a promise is only as good as its maker." The trouble is, most are standing too close to be able to identify it. Others are able to define it but will allow it to change with every expedient until it's dissolved to nothing. Still others prefer to let the company's identity fade into the background and make every brand stand completely on its own image. This, I think, is unfortunate. A product is a thing; a company is human beings.

But the maker's mark, for those companies who recognize its value and whose dedication to it is more than temporary, can put a significant multiplier on the long-range effectiveness of their advertising. At the same time it adds meaning and sub-stance to the implicit contract by personalizing "the party of the first part."

Salesmanship

What we've been talking about thus far is not the stuff that advertising texts are made of, generally speaking. It is basic common sense, easily grasped by all. For advertising is salesmanship and everyone is a salesman. This is why the carping of the professional critics is so difficult to understand and the violation of the implicit contract so difficult to excuse.

No matter what you do in life, your success at it relies heavily on your ability to communicate and explain your point of view to others in a way that will convince them to share it, or at least consider sharing it. This is called persuasion, and every human being is engaged in it constantly. We are married because one or the other party—maybe both—was successful at persuasion. We have our present job as a result of our ability or lack of ability to persuade. A child, a lover or an advertising agency chairman gets to do the things he wants to do on the basis of his ability to persuade.

Regarding the other party as a person rather than as people is an important key to getting through any day with more ease. Addressing someone by name, remembering something that's important to him and asking about it, making that person know you recognize him as an individual rather than a face in the crowd, is going to cause him to respond more positively to you. I watch with admiration as my wife practices this "persons, not people" approach on butchers, dry cleaners, produce managers and service station owners in our town. Recognizing how much better I live as a result, I try to follow the same approach at the office.

Similarly, it's important that the people who come into contact with you recognize you as a unique and consistent entity.

Your "maker's mark" must be apparent, and it cannot change drastically depending on how you feel that day, the particular statement you're trying to make about yourself and society, or, worst of all, the social station of the person you're encountering.

It's important to get the other party nodding in agreement. When you want your husband to put a new washer in the kitchen faucet, you don't say, "Charlie, why can't you be like Rex Lightheart? He's so handy around the house. He wouldn't let a faucet drip for three weeks without lifting a hand." The likely result of approaching the subject this way is that you'll engender an intense hatred of Lightheart within poor Charlie's breast. The opening statement does nothing to prompt Charlie to a positive consideration of what you're asking him to do for you. It does nothing to start him nodding in agreement. In fact, it gets him shaking his head in opposition because he doesn't happen to aspire to Lightheart-edness. He rather likes—or would like to like—himself the way he is.

One thing's certain—you can never persuade someone to your point of view when he's shaking his head. You can only do it when he's nodding.

Much has been written about the insidious powers of advertising. There are none. Paranoids like Vance Packard, author of *The Hidden Persuaders*, have made fortunes peddling the fiction that advertising is some arcane force that causes you to act against your will. It's hogwash. Advertising depends upon the simple precepts of human persuasion. And these have to do, for the most part, with treating the other party as a unique, important individual, letting him recognize your distinct positive identity and starting off by getting him nodding in agreement.

Think of your dealings with your own children. If you've been successful—and to parents that means getting them to accept your values and conduct themselves according to your standards—it undoubtedly is due largely to their knowing exactly who you are, trusting that you aren't going to suddenly metamorphose into someone quite different, and acknowledging that what you are is deserving of a certain respect. It's due also, I daresay, to your recognition of each of them as distinct and

JOHN O'TOOLE

unique human beings from birth, not subhumans grouped into a
category called "kids." And it's probably due, as well, to the fact
that you began each attempt at persuasion in a way that got
them nodding in agreement at the outset—maybe something
like: "It's hard being different, being the one who doesn't do
everything the rest of the crowd does. I'm sure a lot of your
friends are smoking pot, for instance. . . ."

Unless we're hermits, every one of us is faced with persuading a group of our peers at some time or other. We have to get
up before a PTA meeting, a club, a business or union conference or a political gathering and try to sway a number of other
minds, sometimes hostile ones, to our particular point of view.
Here again, the keys to success are the same.

You start out by remembering who you are. The most ineffective speakers are those who, because they're standing before
an audience, feel they have to adopt an alien personality. Simple, straightforward people suddenly become pompous and flow-
ery, the humble become theatrical, and the naturally amusing
become dull. The most important element in public speaking is
to know who you are and speak in a way that is true to yourself.
An audience doesn't buy an idea presented without confidence,
and no one can be confident when he isn't being himself.

Next, you know and you understand and you speak personally and directly to one individual who personifies your audience.
That doesn't mean you rivet some poor soul with an unwavering
stare until he's squirming with discomfort. You simply have
another human being in mind whom you're attempting to persuade
on a one-to-one-basis, and you keep addressing that single person
as your eyes move from face to face in your audience.

Finally, you don't start out telling the group what you want
them to do. It just doesn't work. And the chill hostility it evokes
from an audience is something from which none but the most
adept speaker can recover. But then, an adept speaker doesn't
try it. He talks about what his audience would like to have
happen, then shows how what he wants them to do is the best
way to bring that about. In other words, he gets them nodding
in agreement first.

THE TROUBLE WITH ADVERTISING . . .

Shakespeare weaves for us the account of Henry V preparing his troops for the battle of Agincourt. Being skilled at the techniques of human persuasion, Henry does not plunge into the subject by shouting, "Once more unto the breach, dear friends, once more; or fill the wall up with our English dead." Recognizing this as a rather difficult sale, he saves these forceful words for later. Before the battle he begins by mentioning that it's the feast of St. Crispin. No one can argue with that. Then he states that everyone who takes part in the forthcoming battle will remember and be remembered on St. Crispin's Day "from this day to the ending of the world." Heads begin to nod. He goes on to suggest that "gentlemen in England now abed" who aren't there to participate in the battle will "hold their manhoods cheap" and "think themselves accurs'd they were not here." Heads begin nodding more vigorously. Then, and only then, does Henry start giving battle orders.

Many of us these days spend a good deal of our time writing information to others. The purpose of such written communication is the same as the purpose of most spoken communication: to persuade. We are trying to persuade one or more individuals that our account of an event is interesting or true. If you're writing to a store to tell them that their computer has totally fouled up your billing statement or that the power lawn mower you bought is a real lemon, the purpose of the communication is to make someone pay attention, recognize that it's a real problem, believe you and feel compelled to take some action. If you're writing a memo to an associate or a letter to a customer, if you're writing a classified ad to sell your house or your antique table, or a letter of application to sell yourself to a prospective employer, you're trying to accomplish the same things.

In other words, you want your reader to recognize that you exist (establish your "maker's mark"); you want him to know that you're speaking specifically to him (addressing a person rather than people); you want him opening up to your message at the outset rather than drifting off into negativism or tossing it in a wastebasket (getting him nodding in agreement); you want him to realize that what you're proposing is in his best interests as well as your own ("Hey, he's saying something important to *me*"); and you're doing all this to get him to sell himself on doing something you want him to do (persuasion).

That, essentially, is all there is to it: to persuasion, to selling and to advertising.

PART III

Making
better advertising
while making
advertising better

LEARNING THE STEPS

Every human activity, whether fruitful or frivolous, can be reduced to fundamental steps so that those who do it well and almost instinctively can teach it to those who don't. The latter group may never attain the perfection of the former; then again, they may. But it all begins with the fundamentals.

I have watched Mikhail Baryshnikov teaching a dancer to emulate a series of movements that seemed so natural he might have improvised them. But each step, each position of the arm, head or torso and its relationship to the music, was planned and timed. This much can be taught. The genius lay not in what was done but in how it was done.

Advertising is not dance, but it has its fundamental steps that must be mastered if the result is to have any effect at all. The skill comes in performing each of the steps well. The genius, if if can be called that, comes in making the end result so synchronized, beautifully styled and effortless that the hard work doesn't show.

Misha would forgive my comparing my craft with his art. He, after all, once described basketball to me in ballet terms. And I think that had he been an advertising man and not a dancer—a bizarre thought for someone who grew up in the Soviet Union— he would be just as impatient as I am with people who think they don't have to learn the fundamentals of this craft.

Every month FCB—and, I presume, every other agency— receives a dozen or so unsolicited "ideas" for advertising campaigns. They come from housewives and haberdashers, clergymen and clerks—anyone who has suddenly been visited by an inspiration that will, when "worked out a little," make our client (and the sender) rich beyond dreams of avarice. Nowadays we turn these over to our lawyers the moment we recognize them, unopened if possible, in the event of subsequent lawsuits. And having read some of them in the past, I do so with no sense of loss.

Now, the truth is that one of those forlorn envelopes might contain an idea close to what we eventually come up with, which is why we don't even look at them for fear of being sued. And some evening on the dance floor at Regine's I might accidentally execute a move that looks vaguely like something Baryshnikov did on an off night. But the coincidence is meaningless.

In this section we'll be looking at advertising in terms of the fundamentals. First we'll talk about the three stages of advertising development: strategy, idea and execution. In addition to the development of the advertising message, its delivery is of major importance. This fourth fundamental we call media. The fifth fundamental is the lifeblood of the other four. It represents the essential material from which they are constructed and nourished throughout the sequence. It is loosely and inadequately named research.

That, quite candidly, is all there is to advertising. Now, if you are prepared to accept a few assumptions, we can set off on a purposeful course. First let us assume that Kennedy and Lasker and Hopkins were correct in perceiving that advertising is simply salesmanship. Then let us assume that I am correct in expanding that definition for the 1980s to salesmanship functioning in the paid space and time of mass communication media. Finally—and this is the leap of faith—let us assume that the principles of effective salesmanship, like the articles of the implicit contract, center around an understanding of, an interest in and a respect for the prospect.

If these assumptions are valid, then a discussion of the fundamentals that is rooted in them and guided by them will serve as a kind of blueprint for that happiest of combinations: advertising that makes those who practice it richer while making those who are exposed to it more content.

STRATEGY

"Strategy" is one of those terms that the professional critics are always waving before the public like photos of wartime atrocities. "Look," they say, "how these advertising knaves are conspiring to devise 'strategies' by which to assault your feeble defenses and plunder your pocketbook."

First of all, strategies are devised to assault the competition, not the consumer. Secondly, the word is not only a military term but a sports term as well. In fact, it is much more applicable to advertising in its football sense. Advertising strategies are either defensive or offensive. They are conceived to achieve gains at the expense of the opposing team (the competitive product) a yard (or share point) at a time. When they are successful, the paying fans in the stands get their money's worth and come back for more.

Strategy is the key to success for an advertising campaign. It is not possible to succeed with a brilliant idea and superb execution of the wrong strategy, but it is possible to attain some success with no idea and a dull execution of the right strategy. This becomes painfully apparent almost every time you turn on your television set.

Strategy is information that bright, creative, analytical minds have synthesized and shaped into a sort of master plan for making advertising and developing media plans. The information is research—not the fundamental that goes by the same name, but one of its many aspects that will pop up at every stage of development and beyond. In this initial phase it is composed of market studies, competitive reports, product tests, sales reports, anything and everything written, filmed or taped on the subject. And, at our place, it involves days and days of dialogue with consumers.

While the strategy document itself may be as thick as *War and Peace*, what we generally refer to as strategy is really the answers to these questions:

1. Who or what is the competition for our product or service?
2. Who is the person we're talking to?
3. What must we get that person to know or feel or understand in order to accomplish our objective.

Each of the three steps in advertising development—strategy, idea and execution—requires a distinct kind of creative thinking. Strategy calls for deductive thinking, the kind that characterizes the work of research scientists and fictional private detectives. Sometimes hunches set off down the path of logic only to collapse at the finish line. Other times a flash of insight reveals a unique strategic opportunity. And the deductive "Eureka!" can occur while you're pondering any or all of the three questions.

Who or what is the competition? The answer seems obvious; that's why it can lead to missed opportunities. Generally the competition is similar brands, but not always. Life styles and attitudes can create competitive influences stronger than alternative brand choice. For Master Charge we found there were two groups of people—those with inherited wealth, and foreign-born blue-collar workers—among whom the competition was not so much Bank Americard as the idea of buying anything on credit. We opened up the potential market for Sunkist oranges by broadening the competition from frozen and concentrated juice to snacks in general. In both cases it was talking with consumers that yielded the illuminating insights.

Who is the person we're talking to? It must be clear from all that has gone before that I consider this an extremely important question. This little story illustrates why. When Campbell Soup developed Soup for One, single-serving cans of semicondensed soup, the logical prospect seemed to be the single, divorced or widowed person or the childless couple. It's a sizable market and, what with the state of things today, a growing one. More-over, Lipton was capitalizing on this market with their dry-mix product, Cup of Soup.

The research provided a hunch, insight and logic turned the hunch into a theory, and a quick survey made the theory a foundation of the strategy: there was a much larger market among families with children. And their eating patterns were changing. Family members had different activities and were, more and more, eating at different times. The family meal was fast becoming a memory. Thus, a single-serving soup of excellent quality fit nicely into their new needs. Deciding who we *should* be talking to made all the difference.

Much of the information on which we base our answer to this question is demographic. But, as mentioned earlier on, demographics alone are inadequate. That's why we insist on another look at our prospect, an observation through a different lens. We call it the personal profile. It is actually a subjective analysis of any and all information available on the prospect, including insights gleaned from phone interviews, group sessions and personal experience.

In preparing a story, a journalist will sometimes write a lead in which he tries to dramatize the effect of an event on a representative individual. That individual, while often a product of the journalist's imagination, could well be real. The personal profile is much like this kind of lead. Its purpose is to manufacture out of the dry harvest of statistical analysis a human being with whom we can communicate in personal terms, with whom the group of human beings who are the advertiser can open a dialogue.

The prototypical prospect is given a name, a place to live, a family, a history and a set of attitudes. All of it must make sense. It must be consistent with the information provided by research. It must withstand the test of logic. But it must also project a vital individual presence that becomes the "person" to whom we tailor our communication. At the risk of redundancy, I repeat: advertising works best when it most closely approximates a dialogue between two human beings. In this endeavor, there is no greater aid than crystallizing all available knowledge, understanding and intuition of the other participant in the dialogue into a skillful personal profile.

What must we get that person to know or feel or understand in order to accomplish our objective? If any of the three questions is more important than the others, this is it. And if any is easier to answer wrong, this is it. It seems to me it wasn't always thus. There was a time when products were fewer and life was simpler. The answer to "What do we want someone to take away from our ad?" was often so obvious that only a steadfast dedication to obfuscation could mislead.

For example, in the late fifties we went to work for S.O.S Soap Pads. The product was made of steel wool and soap—that's all. So was the competition, Brillo. Both products were colored pink, and there was no great difference in their sales volume. We went out and asked women which of the two ingredients was more important to them, and they told us it was soap. So we persuaded the client to change the ratio of steel wool to soap in favor of the latter and to make the pads blue instead of pink to call attention to the change. We launched a campaign telling women, "New, blue S.O.S. It's loaded with soap," and took seven points away from the competitor's share of the market.

Yes, that was a simpler era. Today the prospect has many more choices that can be directly or indirectly competitive with our client's product or service. So the right answer to this question depends heavily on a right answer to question 1. Today there are many life-style and attitudinal factors to consider. So the right answer depends even more heavily on a right answer to question 2.

Sometimes the answer comes from the people who make the product, but not always. Albert Lasker said, "Again and again I have seen cases where the thing that interested the manufacturer the least was the very thing that attracted the consumer the most." There's not often such a dramatic dichotomy these days, but getting inside the consumer's head and looking at the product through his eyes usually reveals benefits somewhat different from the ones the manufacturer sees.

When we went to work for the Bermuda Department of Tourism, the answer to question 3 seemed apparent from interviews with many people on the island: "Bermuda offers you breathtaking beauty, unexcelled golf and sailing and sightseeing, plus a charming, civilized environment." All that is true, but it's incomplete. A study of repeat visitors, people who have returned for a second, fifth, even twentieth vacation, uncovered an equally correct answer: "Bermuda offers you the kind of people you want to meet and get to know on your vacation."

Which brings up a problem. What if there is more than one answer to question 3? Strictly speaking, there should not be. An ad or commercial can effectively communicate only one point. If it simply piles unrelated points on top of one another, only one will be remembered—or, more probably, none. But *related* points can often be gathered under a larger concept. In the case of Bermuda, the beauty, the activities, the charm of the island are communicated in every ad—but through the eyes and with the actual words of one of those people or families our prospect would like to meet on his vacation (but this begins to take us into the realm of the idea, which is a later step in advertising development).

So the answer to question 3 must recognize who or what the real competition is, and it must grow out of a deep and personal understanding of the prospect and a thorough but objective view of the product or service. If these conditions obtain, the deductive mind will soon perceive a need, a want, a problem or a dream that, when juxtaposed to one feature of the product or service, locks into it like the final piece of a Chinese puzzle. The result is the "consumer benefit," the only legitimate answer to question 3.

Figuring out strategy is fun. Because it is based on logic and deduction, it is akin to game playing and, properly approached, can provide the same kind of exhilaration. For example, if you're a fan of American football, you will quickly see analogies with advertising strategies, as I said before. And, while the latter usually come without cheerleaders and pom-pom girls, you may be moved to similar enthusiasms when your daring strategy results in a six-point lead over the competition.

In the early seventies it became clear that young women and girls were not only wearing their hair long, they were making some kind of statement with it. It appeared to us that for a certain age and attitudinal group, long hair was becoming their most valued possession. Reviewing all the shampoos and conditioners on the market at the time, we could find none formulated to offer a specific benefit for long hair. There were products promising shiny hair, cleaner hair, more body, less dryness, more manageability and less dandruff, but nothing that would make that girl we were beginning to know say, "That's what I've been waiting for."

We went to our client, Clairol, with an analysis of the market demonstrating this "gap," with tapes of our consumer workshops on the subject, with projections as to how big a business might be developed and how much would have to be spent. And, of course, we took along our strategy, which in this case was really a product we were asking the client to develop—a product designed especially for long hair and the problems that go with it. We had the advertising, the package design and the name: Long & Silky conditioner. A football fan would see that our strategy was a run off tackle. Our quarterback found an opening in the competition's line and handed the ball off to his running back, who took it through the gap before the competition could close up his defense.

Sometimes, to avoid meeting the competition where he chooses and carry the confrontation to a part of the field more advantageous to us, an end run seems in order. When we introduced Sunkist Orange Soda in 1978, we knew something our competitors didn't: the enormous appeal and positive associations the name Sunkist would bring to what would otherwise be one more entry into the crowded and less than dynamic orange sector of the soft drink category. Our strategy was devised to transfer the values inherent in the Sunkist name to the new drink so thoroughly that it would transcend the orange soda category and be considered an alternative to 7-Up, Dr. Pepper, even Pepsi and Coke. That's precisely what happened. While the other orange sodas went into a defensive huddle and the first-string market leaders were off in another stadium pursuing more massive conflicts, Sunkist Orange Soda came off the bench, made an end run around the orange soda line and took over, in city after city, fourth or fifth position in terms of total soft drink sales.

As you fellow fans know, when it's third down and ten and the clock is running out, you've got to take the risk; you go for broke. Usually it's a long pass thrown with as much hope as precision. Sometimes a product gets into a third-and-ten situation and there's nothing to do but go for the "bomb," as it's called. I suspect Arm & Hammer Baking Soda was in that position several years ago. Every American family probably had a package of Arm & Hammer on a shelf somewhere—and probably used it no more than twice a year. Why should they? There's precious little baking from scratch going on these days, and the indigestion market has been taken over by Alka-Seltzer and other such amelioratives. What to do? Throw a long pass and hope someone catches it, someone who happens to be on your team. That's what Arm & Hammer did with a strategy designed to increase frequency of use with unusual new suggestions: open a package and put it in your refrigerator to absorb odors; open another package and pour it down your sink drain to sweeten it.

Then there are times when prudence dictates a predictable, unglamorous strategy rooted in your strengths—simply because those strengths are sufficient to blow foes off the field. My university was never celebrated for its prowess in football, but when Ohio State came to Northwestern each fall it was like the Rape of the Sabines. Woody Hayes and his herd of bull elephants would trample our scholarly group of dilettantes under the most effective running game in the Big Ten. It would have been folly for Ohio State to employ any strategy other than hit-and-run.

Similarly, it would be folly for Sears, Roebuck and Co. to

choose anything but what is called the price-value strategy. They practically own it. Widespread positive attitudes toward Sears are built on the consumer's belief that Sears will not only give him quality merchandise that lasts but will give it to him at a low price. Low price and high quality are, in the consumer's view, easy to find individually but almost impossible to discover in combination. When someone or something can promise that combination and establish over the years that it will be provided consistently and reliably, he has mined the dearest gold in the hills of marketing. The only reason he needs an advertising agency is to keep his own employees from abandoning the price-value strategy.

While this isn't the only function FCB performs for Sears, it is the most important. The desire to fiddle with something that is working is almost irresistible to the human animal. And the impulse to try a new strategy, especially one legitimized by the latest theory of societal evolution, is almost as universal. But an identity like Sears', rooted in and sustained by a price-value strategy, transcends the possible short-term gains of yielding to those impulses and desires. There is only one strategy that makes sense for Sears—and it's not too dissimilar from the one that made such sense for Woody Hayes and his Buckeyes.

No small contributor to the success of Ohio State under Woody Hayes—and the Green Bay Packers under Vince Lombardi—was the concept of positioning. Positioning in football means looking over the teams in the conference (I admit Hayes and Lombardi took a broader view) and determining where you want to be placed, in the view of the public, among those teams. In marketing, positioning is similar but more complex. It means finding the place where the manufacturer wants the consumer to perceive his product in relation to the many other products within a given category. There are often more competitive alternatives for the prospect than there are football teams in a conference, and the standards of evaluation for a category of products are probably more numerous than for a team within a league (though they admittedly hold less emotional intensity).

The standards by which consumers position products in their own minds, however subconsciously, are price, benefits, the importance and exclusivity of those benefits, the emotional property of the product, their firsthand experience with it, what they've heard and read about it—all this judged in the context of what competitive products sell for, offer as benefits and seem to be in terms of personal experience and word of mouth.

The position must, of course, be rooted in the reality of the product; it would be silly for the marketers of the Volkswagen Rabbit to decide they were going to position it as the most luxurious of motorcars. And the position must be read through the eyes of the consumer; no matter how hard Miles Laboratories has tried to position Alka-Seltzer as a headache remedy, consumers insist on viewing it as an effective reliever of upset stomachs. On the other hand, some dramatic repositionings have been pulled off; in the early 1950s, Marlboro was a rather high-fashion cigarette for women.

But repositioning is a drastic step. A successful brand usually has its position firmly set, as reflected not only in the advertising but in the product itself, the packaging and the promotional planning. So positioning is a strategic consideration, and the three basic questions must be answered with the brand's positioning in mind. Should the answers indicate that the positioning of the brand needs to be changed, the job is going to be a major one and will involve more than advertising.

There is one other thought process we use in the strategy stage. We call it executional planning, and its purpose is to fine-tune the strategy in a way that will provide a more accurate direction for the idea and execution. Essentially we are trying to determine whether the answer to question 3 is best accomplished by appealing to the prospect's reason or to his emotions. Most frequently it is a combination of both, and we are trying to arrive at the proper balance.

We do this by constructing a grid whose vertical axis measures the importance of the purchase, with the horizontal axis running from pure thinking on the left to pure feeling on the right. By placing our product on this grid we can usually see the nature of the sale we are trying to make and the direction our idea should take. By placing competitive products on the same grid, we can see whose turf we might be invading with either approach. For example, if we were dealing with the wristwatch category, our grid might look like this:

	thinking	feeling
important	ROLEX	PIAGET
unimportant	TIMEX	CARAVELLE

Both Rolex and Piaget are expensive watches and, one can assume, are important matters to anyone considering their purchase. But Rolex appeals on the basis of thinking. Its features invite the prospect to consider purchase in a rational manner. Piaget costs more and promises esthetics and prestige. Timex and Caravelle are both inexpensive and relatively unimportant purchases. Yet Timex appeals to one's sense of practicality, to reason. Caravelle differentiates itself from Timex by presenting more of a "kicky" buying decision

We can see by this placement whether thinking or feeling should be the primary direction of the message for each brand. We can also see which direction would be most effective if we were trying to make one brand more appealing to the owner of another. A Rolex owner might be persuaded to buy Timex as a second watch on the basis of a serious, thoughtful ad that scales the decision down in importance. Timex might expand its market with an elegant watch pitched emotionally to someone otherwise inclined toward Caravelle.

The thinking/feeling grid is a simple exercise, but it is valuable because it forces a look at the market in terms of the consumer. In fact, all the considerations involved in strategy are only as valuable as the consumer knowledge and understanding that guide them. If the advertising person hasn't moved out of the ivory tower to talk with his prospects, to see his product and its benefits through the prospect's eyes, to understand how the prospect views it in relation to all other products that could conceivably substitute for it, then the strategy will be at least a few degrees off. And that's all it takes for an ad to miss its prospect completely.

IDEA

With the strategy firmly in place to assure us that we'll be saying the right thing to the right person in the right context, and with a little executional planning to adjust our course, we're ready for the next stage of development: getting the idea.

Most advertising texts and advertising people speak in terms of two developmental stages: strategy and execution. Some assume everyone will understand that something creative is to happen in execution, but that's a hazardous assumption. It makes "execution" so vague as to be almost meaningless, which is why I've limited it here to the physical aspects of making ads and commercials, a subject we'll get to at our leisure. The idea stage is too much fun to rush through, and too essential to advertising that both multiplies the effectiveness of the strategy and makes the message more pleasing to the recipient.

Though some assume that execution includes getting an idea, far too many simply execute strategies. The result is usually dull advertising. I am convinced that what consumers have in mind when they label the whole business "boring" is advertising that merely lays out the answer to strategy question 3 on thirty seconds' worth of film or a blank magazine page. I am equally convinced that this kind of advertising produces minimal results for the advertiser—or demands a far greater media expenditure to obtain an effect than does advertising with an idea. And that's why I insist that between strategy and execution there be a stage of development devoted totally to finding that idea.

Now comes the hard part: telling you exactly what an idea is. The best I can do is say it's a flash of insight that synthesizes the purposes of the strategy, that reveals the conjunction of product benefit and consumer desire in a fresh, involving way, that

132

THE TROUBLE WITH ADVERTISING . . .

brings the proposition to life and makes the individual for whom it's intended stop, look and listen. Any definition that long-winded has to be opaque. Perhaps a few examples will clarify it.

Lestoil messages are directed primarily to wives of blue-collar workers, men who are thoughtless enough to get petroleum-based stains on their clothing. The promise is that it will not only help with the toughest cleaning jobs in the house, it will get the toughest stains out of work clothes when used in the laundry. That's the strategy in condensed form. But it's not enough. The strategy must be fueled by an idea that will tempt someone to contemplate such mundane chores, that will make assimilating the message pleasant, that will relate it to the prospect's interests and provide some sort of reward for paying attention. So the writer comes up with such an idea: a woman takes her husband's best workshirt and cleans up the greasiest, messiest parts of the house with it and Lestoil. Now, there's a reason to get involved. How is he going to react to that? What's going to happen to the shirt? Next she launders the shirt with the help of Lestoil. Tension is relieved. It looks terrific. The point has been made as clearly as it could be stated in a strategy document, but with meaning, interest, memorability and drama. That's the difference between a strategy and an idea.

We once had a fishing boat from Sears to advertise. It was called the Gamefisher. Our strategy was to convince sports-minded men, particularly fishing enthusiasts, that the Gamefisher was the *safest* fishing boat they could buy. Our idea was to put big Ted Williams into that boat on a small lake and have him do everything he could to sink it: kick the hell out of it, drill holes in it, even saw it in half. As Ted starts the motor and cruises off in half a Gamefisher, you understand the difference between a strategy and an idea.

I've already mentioned a commercial we did some time back for Hallmark Cards, a two-minute spot that appeared for many years on *The Hallmark Hall of Fame*. It took us through the entire day—one of *those* days—of a young working woman. She misses her bus in the morning and gets to work late, and as is often the case, that triggers off a series of minor frustrations

133

ending with her working late and finally arriving home drenched by a sudden rainstorm. She is met by her cat—and an unexpected Hallmark card that lets her know someone is thinking of her. Perhaps someone she loves. Our strategy for that commercial merely defined our prospect and told us to convince him or her that "someone you love would appreciate receiving a Hallmark card today." That's the difference.

In graphic form, it's the difference between "Convince young children and their mothers that Kool-Aid is fun to prepare as well as drink" and the smiling face that my friend Marvin Potts drew in the condensation on the side of a frosty pitcher of Kool-Aid. In purely verbal form, it's the difference between "Convince suburban and rural homeowners that Raid is the most effective bug killer available" and "Raid kills bugs dead."

Obviously the idea stage calls for a different variety of creative thinking than the strategy stage. If the latter demands deduction, the former requires inspiration. Since inspiration, as Thomas Edison pointed out, is closely associated with perspiration, it's not surprising that many advertising people find ways of avoiding this stage. Since there's no guarantee that inspiration will strike before the deadline, it's little wonder that so many advertisements are delivered to the client without it. But since there are ways of encouraging inspiration to pay us a visit if we understand something about how the creative mind functions, it's worth a little discussion.

Let's start by trying to define creativity in the arts, among which advertising is not. Creativity in the arts is doing the unexpected successfully. Though thoroughly inadequate, this definition at least provides one criterion for separating what is creative from what is not. For instance, Picasso certainly did the unexpected with elating success. So did W. H. Auden. And Igor Stravinsky. On the other hand, Norman Rockwell and Edgar A. Guest and John Philip Sousa did the *expected* successfully. So their work is not creative art.

Now let's see how the definition applies to creativity in the crafts, which is the proper category for advertising. Here I would narrow it to doing the unexpected successfully within more rigid and utilitarian parameters. What Dashiell Hammett did within the conventions of the detective mystery, and what Red Smith does within the disipline of sports reporting, are examples of creativity in the crafts. Given the standard ballad form, so are what Burt Bacharach does with music and what Lorenz Hart did with lyrics and what Cole Porter did with both. So are what Wright did with the dwelling and Eames with the chair. But according to that definition, other craftworks are not creative. Most television series today are craftworks and operate within the parameters of time and budget. Some are commercial and popular successes. Few are unexpected.

So, if we are going to understand what is creative in the craft of advertising, we have to recognize its utilitarian parameters. And to do this, we have to understand that advertising is really the craft of salesmanship. The fact that we exploit photography, art, prose and cinematography in advertising should not delude anyone into thinking that the vast boundaries of those arts extend to our craft or its utilitarian purpose. It is not Faulkner or Fellini to whom we look for creative guidelines, but those great drummers and door-beaters and merchants of old who probed the more prosaic limits within which they could do the unexpected successfully.

It is that unremembered door-to-door vacuum cleaner salesman who first thought of demonstrating the powers of his machine by showing the lady how much dirt it could pull out of the mattress she thought was perfectly clean. It is the anonymous beer salesman who stopped at the roadside inns of my youth to put this little sign at eye level above the urinal:

> Now you can enjoy
> another bottle
> of Stroh's Beer.

Old masters like these did the unexpected in order to achieve an immediate exchange of money for product.

Since advertising is salesmanship functioning in the paid space and time of mass communication media, its objective is to persuade a certain kind of person to make a mental commitment to exchange money for product at the next opportunity. This goal, the strategy, the inherent limitations of the various media, and the prospect's haste, preoccupation, cynicism, indifference and caution are some of the parameters within which advertising must do the unexpected successfully if it is to be creative. This is the job of the idea.

It's not easy. But when it works, magical things happen. Sometimes the prospect experiences a shock of recognition. Because of the way the information has been presented, he perceives in a burst of illumination that the message has to do with him and his life; it's a key that fits snugly into the lock of a need he has or a problem he didn't even realize he had. During the 1975 recession, an ad for Kraft Dinners did just that. It featured a clean, appetizing down-shot of the prepared dish, with the headline "How to eat well in spite of it all."

To introduce Levi's Jeans for Men we did a radio commercial that used simple narration by a man out jogging. He says that despite the good shape he's in, nature has redistributed his weight and boys' jeans just aren't right for him anymore. He wants a higher rise and "a skosh more room in the thighs." We figured the men who were our prospects would keep themselves in decent shape or they wouldn't fit into jeans. Furthermore, we figured many would have put in some military service between 1950 and 1960—a time when the term "skosh" (derived from the Japanese *sukoshi* and meaning "little") was in monotonous currency. Judging from the mail that came in, as well as the sales, that idea produced a shock of recognition.

I mentioned the idea we came up with for S.O.S. Soap Pads in the fifties: loaded with soap. It's an idea, but a little underweight. We needed something more audacious, an idea that would produce a shock of recognition—particularly in New York City, where almost 25% of the nation's soap pads were purchased, and where Brillo outsold S.O.S. six to one. For some reason, Jewish housewives seemed to use an inordinate number of the things. That was enough to conjure up a vision of Gertrude Berg, star of *The Goldbergs*, putting an S.O.S. pad in her mixmaster to demonstrate the enormous quantity of suds it produced. We persuaded her to do it, and as the suds cascaded over her kitchen table and piled up on the floor, she exclaimed, "Look! With soap it's loaded." S.O.S. sales doubled.

Another kind of idea can create a simulated experience. Sampling is the best method of selling a good product, but the closest we can come to it in our craft is the simulated experience that certain ideas can make happen. A good demonstration idea often produces such an experience. For example, a Sears ad shows a model scrunched up within the spatial confines of the page wearing Pants-that-Fit to demonstrate the fabric's flexibility. A woman can almost feel the "give" in the garment. Another Sears commercial, one for the DieHard battery, depicts five cars with dead batteries being started with a single two-year-old DieHard. As those engines growl and come to life, a man almost sighs with relief. Such simulation can be accomplished through empathy as well. Women "experience" the product when they see a Lady Clairol ad describing what it's like to become a blond. You yourself have probably "tasted" the rich, moist cake in a well-photographed cake mix ad.

When we do the unexpected successfully within our utilitarian parameters, more prospects are stopped by the message and perceive its application to their own lives. More participate in a simulated experience of the product; more remember it; more make a mental commitment to try it. But how is this achieved?

An advertising notable named James Webb Young published a little volume in 1940 called *A Technique for Producing Ideas*, in which he theorized that creativity means forming new combinations of old elements and depends on an individual's ability to perceive new relationships. When I read that I was reminded of an incident in Albert Lasker's book *Salesmanship in Print*. After describing how John Kennedy rewrote a mail order ad for a washing machine, Lasker said that whereas the manufacturer had been spending as much as $20 in media to elicit each response to the original ad, Kennedy's rewrite brought the cost down to a few pennies.

Here's what Kennedy did. Like most expensive products of the time, the machine was sold on the installment plan: $2.00

down and $2.00 a week for a total of $12.00. Kennedy explained in the copy that a woman's time was worth at least $1.20 a day because that's what she'd pay a laundress. Since the machine did a day's work in half a day, it would save her $.60 a day. So he said, "Try it for four weeks at my expense. Whatever the savings are, keep them all for yourself. But after that, send me 50 of the 60 cents you save for 24 weeks. From that time on, the machine is yours." The headline read, "Let This Washing Machine Pay for Itself." This isn't something we'd want to try today, but you must admit it's an example of forming new combinations of old elements by perceiving new relationships.

A more recent example is an ad from a series for Johnson Controls, the nation's largest manufacturer of electronic systems for buildings. The first element that stops the eye is an artwork illustration of a large apartment building. In the next instant the eye notes that the building looks very much like a radiator. Then it lights on the headline, "12 ways to tell if your modern building is squandering costly energy." The key that draws legitimate prospects into the ad is a perceived relationship between a building that's wasting heat and a radiator. The new combination of old elements derived from that perception makes a building owner see the application to his own problem and experience an urgency about reading the proposed solution.

Obviously creativity isn't a totally rational thought process, which may be why more psychiatrists have written about it than advertising men. Freud, for example, in a number of studies on the subject, concludes in essence that creativity is "regression in the service of the ego" and that the creative person is a frustrated, neurotic and sexually unfulfilled individual who creates as a means of sublimation (if that were all it took, advertising agencies would be overflowing with creative ideas). There are many more theories, most of which boil down to an elementary conflict or tension between two portions or faculties of the mind: the id and the ego, the left and right hemispheres of the brain, lateral and linear thinking, and so on.

Among these many formulations, I have found useful the view presented by Dr. Silvano Arieti in *Creativity, the Magic*

Synthesis. Arieti starts with the distinction made by others between primary process and secondary process thinking. Primary process is the kind of thinking that occurs in dreams and in children before we worry it out of them. It is primitive and illogical. Secondary process thinking is orderly and analytical. It is learned. Arieti believes that creativity is "the magic synthesis" of the two processes, the ability to dip from time to time into the irrational process while proceeding along the rational course, thus emerging with what James Webb Young would call "new combinations."

According to Arieti, this synthesis is what produces new and startling metaphors for the poet. It is also, I believe, what produces new and startling metaphors in advertising. It is what led one of our copywriters in London to see a relationship that resulted in this concept for a moisturizing skin cream called Astral: "The soft drink for your skin." It is what led another in Sweden, working on Volkswagen, to combine a photograph of a man in shoes far too large for him with the line "If Swedes bought shoes the way they buy cars . . ." And I can see now that it's what led me, some years ago when I worked in Los Angeles, to perceive the relationship between a guarantee and the word Sunkist stamped on an orange; thus, "Our guarantee is printed on the back of every package."

How much primary process thinking should go into the mix, and how much secondary? I suppose most failures could be chalked up to too little secondary process, but I can think of a number of successful ads that I can honestly explain only in terms of primary process thinking. One features a beguiling little boy happily dipping into a bag of Kraft Marshmallows, with the headline "A marshmallow a day keeps your freckles on straight." Another for Veuve du Vernay Sparkling Wine shows a close-up of hands working at the foil, wire and cork that separate us from such pleasant products. The headline: "It's trying just as hard to get out as you are to get in."

There's something to be learned, although I'm not quite sure what, in the evolution of that headline. Veuve du Vernay is not a champagne but a less expensive sparkling wine imported from

France into England. The strategy, abbreviated, was this: the competition is liquor and beer, the prospect is a blue-collar worker; what we want to say is that his guests will be flattered and the party more festive if he serves Veuve du Vernay.

After several blind alleys, the creative group in London started down the route of how sparkling wine uplifts and excites both the people and the occasion. It's not just drinking it but opening and serving it. In fact, the moment to concentrate on, the moment that distinguishes this kind of product from the competition, the moment when the consumer benefit is most manifest, is the moment when the prospect is straining to open the bottle—the instant of tension before the cork pops.

With that, the hard part was behind them. They had what is called the "concept." And, as though to prove that it was the right one, headlines flowed from it like—well, sparkling wine. Here's the progression of lines as they occurred:

> "The agony is worth the ecstasy."
> "Good things seldom come easily."
> "It's trying just as hard to get out as you are to get in."
> "Tear back the gold part, unwind the wire part, remove the noisy part and you've arrived at the best part."
> "Before any great opening there's always a little tension."
> "A little business before pleasure."

All those headlines are right. All are totally on strategy. All add the extra dimension of an idea. But something makes the third one, to my mind, more right—more of a simulated experience. And that something is not to be found, or defended, by secondary process thinking.

There's one more process that has a lot to do with creativity in our craft, and that's selective reduction; taking elements out, combining several into one, reducing the density so that it can be filled in by the prospect's own participation. Selective reduction is how we arrived at a spread for Kent cigarettes that shows

140

one package opened at the top with the filters exposed, another upside down and opened at the bottom with the tobacco ends exposed. It says, "Come for the filter. You'll stay for the taste." Then there's a poster we did for the U.S. Forest Service. The verbal message is simply the slogan "Please be careful with fire." But it's on a charred wooden sign.

Well, those are attempts at making clear what an idea is. Once you know how to relax and let it happen to you, an idea is not a rare accomplishment. But an idea that grows directly from the strategy, whose relevance and pertinence derive from that of the product, whose brilliance illuminates in a fresh way the point where consumer want and product feature meet—that's rare. And precious.

And it can still be ruined in the hands of someone who doesn't understand execution.

EXECUTION

Execution is the physical phase of advertising development. It is the handwork, the craftsmanship. It is making something tangible out of the strategy-based idea: a page, a film, a length of audiotape or videotape that represents the message. It involves a kind of creative thinking somewhat different from the deduction that characterizes the strategy stage and the inspiration upon which the idea stage depends. Execution calls for taste. Successful execution demands the skills and esthetic discrimination of the master craftsman.

The tools vary with each medium. In newspapers, magazines, and posters, we work essentially with printed words, photographs and drawings. In radio, we use spoken words, music and sounds. Television uses all of these and adds motion to the photographs and drawings. Television's tool kit is the fullest of all; its combinations are probably infinite.

The purpose of execution in any medium is to transmit the idea and its attendant information to the intended prospect as clearly, quickly and easily as possible. In this stage, as in the other two, the purpose cannot be achieved at all without a real understanding of that prospect, and it cannot be achieved to maximum effect outside the boundaries of the implicit contract. The hallmarks of truly professional execution are simplicity, drama and appropriateness.

Nothing is less simple to achieve than simplicity. Yet we owe it to that prospect of ours to make our presence known in a pleasant way and convey our information as effortlessly as possible. What good salesman would do otherwise? After all, no one is paying the prospect to figure out what we're trying to say. Simplicity demands reducing the number of elements in

142

the message to an absolute minimum and unifying them in a way that not only presents the least formidable journey through the information but makes instantly clear the path to be followed.

Drama means maintaining or enhancing the inherent interest and impact of the idea. Execution should focus on the revelation, the shock of recognition that demonstrates the fusion of product feature and the prospect's own life.

Appropriateness is merely selecting the right tools for the job. You would not sell an emerald necklace with Franklin Gothic Bold, the typeface newspapers use for declarations of war. You would not use jingles and animated cartoons to promote a chain of mortuaries. And it requires further discretion to reflect the maker's mark in the message.

Application of these standards calls for a different combination of skills in each medium. Let's begin with posters since they were the first form of advertising. Because it is something the prospect will generally just glance at while walking or driving by, the poster must involve and communicate instantly. Thus it must, above all, be simple in execution. Secondarily but importantly, it should be dramatic and appropriate.

Poster execution can involve only a picture, though this is rare; so much meaning has been packed into Smokey the Bear that his picture alone is enough to make campers exercise caution with fire, but it's taken almost forty years of advertising to accomplish such immediate results. Poster communications are sometimes purely verbal; the three simple words "Sale ends today" can boost a store's business.

But most frequently poster execution involves both words and pictures. And the most successful posters are composed of just three elements: a picture, a set of words that works with it to make the idea explode, and the identification of the advertiser with either words or picture. A classic example is the picture of a smiling American Indian who has just taken a bite from a slice of rye bread. The words: "You don't have to be Jewish to love Levy's real Jewish Rye." Another poster, which reduces the number of elements even further, shows a large orange with the Sunkist stamp and the line "You have our word on it." The

Levy's example notwithstanding, verbal statements on posters should be brief—never more than seven words.

Magazine and newspaper execution must also strive for simplicity. Whereas in posters simplicity means reducing the number of elements to a minimum, in the press it involves integrating and unifying elements. All our studies have shown this to be the single most important executional consideration in stopping a real prospect. Therefore it is the first function of the layout. The second is to provide an obvious and easy flow through the elements in the sequence in which we want them noted.

Illustrations can be either photographs or artwork, depending on the job to be done; research shows no particular advantage of one over the other. The illustration must, however, communicate the product or the service benefit simply, dramatically and appropriately. Our research shows that ads with large illustrations stop more readers than those with smaller pictures or no pictures. In fact, ads that scored in the top third of our tests for stopping power devoted an average 82% of their space to illustration. Research also confirms that full-color ads were well worth the additional cost over black-and-white in proven consumer response.

The verbal parts of an advertisement are usually the headline, the themeline and the copy. The *headline*, working alone or in conjunction with the major illustration and the layout, should convey information that produces the response "Hey, they're talking to me. They're saying something important to me." If it fulfills that requirement, the number of words will have no bearing. Nor will the positioning of the headline on the page. The only mechanical factors that can decrease recall and comprehension are type that is too large and aggressive, and tricky or mixed typefaces. Headlines, by the way, should always be set in capitals and lowercase, not all capitals.

If the headline doesn't offer any information, it's going to suffer in recall and readership; Gallup & Robinson gives a 12% recall premium to specific headlines and an 11% penalty to vague or "teaser" headlines. And if it doesn't involve the pros-

pect emotionally, both Gallup & Robinson and my experience
say it will be less effective than one that does.

Despite what you may have heard, the use of "you" or "yours"
in a headline does not increase readership. Nor does naming the
advertiser. Nor does the use of "new." If there is newness or
uniqueness in the benefit, the prospect will see it. If not, the
word "new" will convince no one.

Headlines should be vigorous. I inveigh against the passive
voice. I rejoice in active verbs. Why say, as one ad did, "To
BMW enthusiasts, praise like this is taken for granted" when
you could have said, "BMW enthusiasts take praise like this for
granted"? The latter is simpler, livelier, less phoney.

Headlines should sing. They should employ some of the
poet's tools to make them enjoyable to read and easy to remember. Alliteration, for example, is an acknowledged aid to
memorability. My old friend the great FCB copywriter Bob
Koretz wrote the headline "Which twin has the Toni?" in 1946.
It hasn't appeared in the advertising since 1953, yet it's still
remembered today. Back in 1959 I did a campaign for Delsey
Bathroom Tissue built around the headline "There's a definite
difference in Delsey." The campaign ran for only six months,
but I still hear people play that line back at the mention of the
word Delsey.

Which reminds me that it is often easier to put alliteration
into a headline than to keep it there. The brand manager in
charge of Delsey for Kimberly-Clark at the time fought furi-
ously to make me change that line to "There's an important
difference in Delsey." There's some solace in knowing that this
kind of insensitivity is not unique to advertising. The novels
Black Boy and *Run River* were originally to be titled *American
Hunger* and *In the Night Season*. In fact, for one of his novels, F.
Scott Fitzgerald himself submitted the titles *Trimalchio in East
Egg, The Highbouncing Lover* and *Under the Red, White and Blue*.
His publisher fought for, and got, *The Great Gatsby*.

Along with alliteration, an interesting rhythm helps readers
assimilate, feel and remember a headline. One of the most
beautiful headlines I can recall, and the only one I know of in

iambic pentameter, was done by Ogilvy & Mather's Clifford Field for British Tourism. The subject was Westminster Abbey, and the line read, "Tread softly past the long, long sleep of kings."

While headlines should march, dance or skip with effortless grace, memorable cadence and revelatory insight, they should also be short. They should not confront the reader with too imposing a mass of display type. He does not happen upon that page with a lifelong fascination for the product or a zealous determination to comprehend. The shorter the better.

I once saw a trade ad offering Polaroid cameras for use by advertisers as premiums. The illustration was a camera. The headline was "I am a premium." That unknown copywriter, who deserves a special place in the hagiography of our craft, must have worked his pencil to a nub deleting the word "now" at each step of the approval process.

On the other hand, the addition of one word can sometimes work magic. I once read a story about the making of *Gone with the Wind*. Concerning what may be the most quoted line of dialogue in the history of film, the writer said, "In the novel, Rhett's line is 'My dear, I don't give a damn,' but [the] added 'Frankly' was left in, a minor yet incalculable improvement." The day before reading that, I had been interviewing a copywriter. Among her samples was an ad for an English gin that had been advertised with the line "To make martinis with." Upon getting the assignment, she had added one word. The headline became "To make martinis with, luv." (We hired her.)

Headlines should be involving. Fifteen years ago I saw an ad that fascinated me both as a consumer and as a practitioner of the craft. The subject was an imported cheese, and the headline read, "Pâté costs more than liverwurst. Bisque costs more than soup. Stroganoff costs more than stew. This cheese costs more than other Edam. Life is short." The illustration had stopped me with the appetite appeal of the cheese. But the headline had involved me, an even more difficult feat. It had made me participate.

There are several steps of logic that could have been inserted between the last two lines, but more was gained than lost by their omission. For one thing, I had a sudden recognition that the advertiser was a human entity who obviously felt I was too. Equally important, he jarred me with the omission and made me participate in his ad by inviting me to bridge the logic gap myself. A dialogue was in progress, and I eagerly read every word of body copy.

If you know and understand your prospect well enough and your inner ear is sufficiently developed, you can begin leaving gaps and almost hear them being filled in. A poster for the U.S. Forest Service simply shows Smokey the Bear looking at us and saying, "Repeat after me: Only you . . ." On many occasions we have used only the first half of the line "Aren't you glad you use Dial soap? Don't you wish everybody did?" Viewers and readers automatically fill in the second half.

Themelines usually, but not always, make a different statement than headlines make. The themeline is a broader statement of the campaign idea or sometimes of the maker's mark. Headlines change from advertisement to advertisement during the course of a campaign. Themelines endure, tie ads together into a campaign, unite messages in different media into one effort and sometimes display the continuity of an advertiser from campaign to campaign, from product to product, over decades.

The themeline usually appears at the bottom of the ad under the advertiser's signature. Some well-known examples are "When you care enough to send the very best," "At Zenith, the quality goes in before the name goes on," and "Fly the friendly skies of United." The writer of a themeline should recognize that he's crafting something of greater permanence, less specificity and broader application than a headline, but he should be guided by the same executional principles that pertain to headlines.

Copy, sometimes called body copy or text, generally receives too little attention. This is unfortunate, because the copy is where the really interested reader ends up; it's where the substantive and more detailed information is communicated; it's where the sale is made. There are several attributes that are almost invariably present in the body copy of ads judged successful by measured response.

1. A personal, one-to-one style
2. Logical order, leading off with a statement with which the prospect can nod in agreement, and concluding with an exhortation to action
3. Clear, vigorous, grammatical writing
4. Lean, conscientiously edited prose

Length of copy makes no difference in the recall scores accumulated by Gallup & Robinson. Indeed, more information is always better than less, especially for considered purchases as opposed to impulse items. And particularly since, in the era of the thirty-second commercial, ample information is a unique strength of print advertising.

In long-copy ads, the important considerations are simplicity and integration. Information must be ample, but ordered and condensed for maximum ease of assimilation. To achieve this result, the prerequisites are the mind, enthusiasm and talent of a good writer. Then a few mechanical aids will help.

1. A short lead paragraph
2. Lead sentence in boldface
3. Subheads for key points
4. Small, illustrative visuals
5. Indented paragraphs

This is not to say that copy must always be presented in a highly structured traditional format. We've had great success with the "call-out" technique, where information is broken up into discrete units related to an illustration of the product by thin lines. Picture captions are consistently high in readership and are an excellent way to communicate points that warrant more attention than they might receive in a copy block or that deserve to be repeated and expanded upon. What's important is that the presentation be simple and make sense at first glance, and that the prose be written clearly, informatively, interestingly, powerfully, persuasively, dramatically, memorably and with effortless grace. That's all.

Here are a few final executional observations about copy, gained from poring over hundreds of readership studies and watching, for a long time, what works and what doesn't.

> 1. Always set copy in a serif typeface. The type you're reading now has serifs, tiny horizontal lines at the tops and bottoms of the vertical strokes of the letters. Serifs make reading easier. Sans-serif type removes them to achieve a modern effect. Why make it harder in any way for the prospect to absorb the information?
>
> 2. Never make the column of type more than 55 characters wide.
>
> 3. Never surprint text on pictorial matter unless the latter has been airbrushed or treated so as to form a light, single-tone background.
>
> 4. Do not reverse text (white letters on black or full-color backgrounds) under any circumstances.

Those hardy readers who have been paying attention through this unavoidably detail-laden section will have seen that execution in the print media is based on the same fundamental as are strategy and idea: salesmanship. Any successful salesman will work hard to make the entire encounter as easy, pleasant and brief for his prospect as possible.

The same is true of execution in the broadcast media, with some differences of emphasis. For example, radio and television need not strive for brevity. The length of the message is predetermined, usually thirty seconds in television and sixty in radio. Furthermore, a broadcast message is sequential by nature, whereas a printed page presents itself in its entirety, to be accepted or rejected as a whole. Thus a broadcast message is more like a salesman's presentation than is a print advertisement. It is easier to construct than a print advertisement because the more beguiling elements can engage and lead the prospect into the nuts and bolts before he is aware there are nuts and bolts. As a result, while simplicity is important in terms of registering the information and avoiding confusion, drama is the primary consideration in radio and television execution. Simplicity and appropriateness follow closely.

Radio's toolbox offers so few executional implements that it truly separates the rookie from the professional. From earth, water and fire, one person will produce an Etruscan urn, and another warm mud pies. From words, sounds and music, one advertising person will craft an arresting, informative and persuasive piece of radio salesmanship, and another an interval of sound whose vibrations never travel beyond the prospect's eardrum.

The words in a radio commercial must be spare, colorful and lively, just as in print execution. But they should also *sound* like what they designate, for the ear is the only active organ at the receiving end. For example, the adjective "flowing" might be sufficient to modify "gown" in print or television, where an accompanying visual bears the burden. But radio calls for words like "shimmering," "liquescent," "whispering," with sibilant consonants that actually create the sound of the dress in motion. It's called onomatopoeia in poetry. In radio execution it's called painting word pictures.

Words in radio execution should be kept to a minimum and delivered at a pace that recognizes that the recipient has little motivation to struggle in order to keep up. And words should be put together with an awareness of radio's power to excite mental images unfettered by the restraints of realistic graphic interpretation. I can't imagine the most skillful print or television writer creating a piece of communication that would convince thousands of people that visitors from another planet were actually invading New Jersey. But Orson Welles did it in his radio broadcast "War of the Worlds" in 1938:

In a demonstration commercial for the Radio Advertising Bureau, Stan Freberg described, and rather convincingly, the Army Corps of Engineers draining Lake Michigan and filling it with ice cream, chocolate sauce and whipped cream to turn it into a monstrous sundae. By the time the crane lowered a giant maraschino cherry into place, the picture was vivid in the listener's mind. As Stan said in conclusion, "Try that on your television set." Sound effects helped Freberg immensely in bringing verisimilitude to his zany description. Sounds are limited only by the ability of electronic communication to transmit them identifiably. If the sound isn't immediately recognizable, it shouldn't be used.

Music is the least specific of our executional tools for radio, and the one used most subjectively. Little research exists on the effects of music in advertising, and none is convincing. Still, our experience tells us that in many cases it communicates emotionally in a faster and richer way than could words or pictures. I would add, however, that when it's used in combination with words, it must be subordinate. The most common executional transgression against the implicit contract is obscuring the words with too heavy a sound track or burying important words in incomprehensible lyrics. If you want the words to be heard, have them said, not sung. If they must be sung, use one voice, not a chorus. And never, never have them sung by a chorus of children.

And so we arrive at last at the subject of television execution, having already discussed most of its basic tools in terms of their application to other media. In the necessarily abbreviated manner in which we're dealing with them here, the principles stated above for words, sound and music have much the same application to television as to radio. Pictures, of course, take on a different meaning than they have in print media, although the question of whether they're drawings or photographs still has no direct bearing on their efficacy. But using one or the other inappropriately might.

The reason television pictures function differently from those in print seems obvious. Because they move, right? Wrong. Still shots are used in many commercials. A camera can be locked on the product for thirty seconds while an announcer talks. It is not movement per se that distinguishes television execution but its inexorable sequentiality. Time is the additional and magical executional tool of television.

151

JOHN O'TOOLE

Time is a consideration in radio, but not truly a tool. The actual tools of radio are so few and so dominant that they limit and formalize the uses of time. In television, however, the combination of visual factors with audio, multiplied by all the tricks that can be done with time, offers an infinite and as yet barely explored range of executional possibilities. This makes even more shameful the numbing sameness of so many commercials you see on the air each evening.

It's true that most pictures move in a television commercial, but seldom do they move through time at the pace of reality. The most common device to speed time is to "dissolve" or eliminate it. We go from one scene to another with an optical effect that signals, "This is happening some time later." In the seventies we learned how to do this with a simple "cut" from one scene to the next. We can also move time faster by "under-cranking," or shooting fewer frames per second so that time will move through the projector faster. Or we can slow time down to virtually any pace we choose by "overcranking." We can edit out pieces of the action so that people or objects pop magically from one place to another. And we can separate the subject and its background and do any of these things to either simultaneously.

These are just a rudimentary few of the feats of optical and special effects legerdemain that make time our tool in the visual aspect of television. When you combine them with the fact that similar sleight of hand (or sleight of ear) can be performed with the sound, executional possibilities multiply geometrically.

Just being able to put sight and sound together in ways that do not occur in real life opens virgin vistas. The juxtaposition of a picture track and a seemingly unrelated sound track can put another stage on the rocket of the idea. A few years ago, when British Airways introduced its Concorde service between London and New York, we did a special commercial to announce it in the United Kingdom. If you had turned off the sound, you would have seen the camera exploring the astonishingly graceful contours of the aircraft as it prepared for flight, the dramatic takeoff and air-to-air photography as it soared above the clouds. Not a bad visual message. The sound track was a dated rendition of "Give My Regards to Broadway." The implausible combination clicked. The idea exploded. The connotations glowed like embers.

Our ability to combine visual and audio stimuli in infinite varieties through flexible sequences of perceived time makes television execution—quite understandably—an irresistible playground for the neophyte. And therein lies the peril. Too frequently television execution is used as a substitute for an idea, even for a strategy. This is not only the sign of a rookie at work, but it eventually offends the viewer, who knows full well he's watching a commercial and expects, in addition to the pyrotechnics, some kind of information that might have to do with his life.

For a while advertising could coast along on the assurance given by some "reverse-snob" journalists that commercials were more fun to watch than the programs. Though flattering, the observation was irrelevant. Commercials have a mercantile end, and today's more practical-minded viewer knows it. There are other places, the local movie theater for one, to hie to in quest of the latest exploration into filmic experimentation for art's sake. The purpose of television execution is identical to that of print, radio and poster execution: to communicate, as quickly and effortlessly as possible to the individual who is the prospect, the strategy-based idea of the message. A harried and hurried, hopeful yet worried, ordinary human being is the audience—not the Motion Picture Academy of Arts and Sciences.

I realize that throughout this section on execution I have glossed over the subject of illustration, but it is an immense river with many tributaries, an excursion down any of which would cost too many pages. Still, I'm compelled to add a final word about a sub-tool that is important enough to warrant a brief digression: models in advertising.

Flip through any consumer magazine and notice, in so many advertisements, the grinning housewife, the tense housewife, the smug housewife and the enraptured housewife. See her with her plastic family in their pleasure and pain, in their sickness and health. Then pick up a book like *The Best of Life* and study the work of such photographers as George Silk, Gordon Parks, Eugene Smith, Eliot Elisofon and Yale Joel. Observe, in similarly mundane pursuits, human beings whose joy and anguish, whose irritation with and love for one another, are undeniably authentic.

I'm constantly confounded by this contrast. And further confounded when I discover that some of the advertising illustrations have been shot by the same photographers who capture life so beautifully in their noncommercial work. So here are a few executional rules I've developed and promulgated concerning the use of models.

1. Don't insist on flawless beauty in your models. You probably married a slightly large nose or a less than perfect chin, and that's certainly a weightier commitment than you're asking of the reader. Do look for a spirit, an inner light shining through. Look for a person behind the face.

2. Approach retouching warily, especially faces. The retoucher's brush, like the volume control on a hi-fi set, is an implement few seem able to use with restraint. Before you can say "fake," you've traded a marginally imperfect photograph for a thoroughly ghastly painting.

3. Avoid exaggeration. Out there in the real world people seldom grin at products. Very few of my acquaintances gasp in open-mouthed admiration at my purchases or double up in excruciating guffaws at my humor. Such excesses repel the reader's eye in that crucial split second when it first hits the page.

4. A carefully staged situation involving several models will not communicate as real. You're much better off, after setting it up, having one or all of the models look right into the camera, frankly acknowledging its presence. This initiates a personal relationship with the reader that will be far more effective

than your best attempt to convince him the event actually occurred.

5. Don't try to fill every fold and wrinkle with light. If God wanted people lit from every angle, He wouldn't have been so frugal with suns.

6. Finally, be sensitive to your models on a shoot. Make them feel at ease. Listen to them. If what you're asking makes them feel foolish, what you'll see in the contact prints will most likely have the same effect on you.

So much for execution. Advertising is characterized by deadlines, and deadlines are imposed by media, and media is our next subject.

MEDIA

Media (a plural noun that takes a singular verb when it refers to a subject or a department) is concerned with selecting the most effective system of delivering the message to the prospect at the lowest possible cost. Media planning is a balancing act. Within the confines of a given budget, a staggering number of considerations must be studied, assigned some sort of numerical weight reflecting the importance of each, and harmonized with the objectives of the marketing plan.

For example, the prospect group for a product might be divided into five subgroups, each having a different level of importance. The message might be suited to five media—television, magazines, newspapers, radio and outdoor (an industry term for all the posters and painted displays seen on billboards large and small, lighted and unlighted, moving or still, along roads or on sides of buildings)—but it might be suited to each to differing degrees, and there might be sharply differing values to be obtained by the first, second, third, fourth and fifth repetitions in each medium. We already have 5 x 5 x 5—or 125—judgments to be made. And that's before considering geography or the characteristics of individual magazines, stations and networks. Little wonder the computer has become the tool of the trade.

We're not going to get into higher mathematics here. We're just going to get acquainted with the major considerations that must be part of any worthwhile media plan, keeping in mind the obligations imposed by the implicit contract. A good place to start is with the media themselves. Each communicates with its audience in a different way, and those differences are critical in deciding which medium will most effectively carry the message, or which combination will provide the optimum overall communication. Let's examine eight considerations that stem from the nature of the media and the different ways in which they work.

Consider, for example, the question of *reaching a mass audience versus reaching a selective group*. Network television attracts a mass audience, an audience that reveals little to us in terms of its attitudes or the way it lives or, for that matter, what would "insult its intelligence." Spot television on a local station offers a heterogeneous audience in a specific geographic location. So does outdoor. Radio selects geographically, too, but also lets us choose among the groups represented by the audiences for country-and-western, top 40, all-news, classical or easy-listening formats. Newspapers are geographically selective. Magazines are most selective of all, each providing an audience that is relatively discrete in terms of interests and life style. And some magazines, such as *Reader's Digest* and *TV Guide*, attract so many readers that the audience numbers come close to those achieved by network television, which brings us full circle.

Why is all this important? Because some products find most of their prospects in certain areas of the country, or more in cities than in rural areas. Some products, such as Bermuda, appeal most to a certain kind of person within a certain income group within a certain geographical area. For Fritos Brand corn chips, on the other hand, everyone in the country is a prospect. For a motorcycle, we would want to reach young men; for Clairol's Loving Care, we want to talk to women over thirty. It's important, too, because sometimes we want to let as many people as possible know about a new product very quickly, which means network television. Other times we may want to add more information to that awareness, especially in a certain part of the country or among people who live a certain way. That calls for newspapers or magazines.

A second consideration is *the kind of interest the prospect brings to the medium*, which will have some bearing on the prospect's frame of mind when he encounters our message. A man may be a regular reader of both *Scientific American* and *Playboy*. When he's reading *Scientific American*, he's going to be seriously seeking intellectual stimulation and hard information. With *Playboy*, he'll probably be more hedonistic and more open to the pursuit of prestigious possessions. Magazine readers will usually have a relatively high intensity of interest because they have sought out and paid for the medium. To a lesser degree, the same is true of newspaper readers; and we can be sure of their having a local interest. Little intensity of interest can be counted on in the television viewer or radio listener, and even less when it comes to the recipient of an outdoor message.

Another consideration that should strongly influence media choice for a particular message is *degree of intrusion*. In a newspaper or magazine, the reader knows an advertisement is there on the page. He makes his own determination, based on what he gleans in the split second his eye encounters the ad, as to whether he'll spend time on it or not. Radio and television do not offer the prospect such a choice and are therefore highly intrusive advertising vehicles (it has been said that this makes them preferable for products of low inherent interest—an undeniable fact that is also a refuge for advertising people of low inherent skill).

A consideration that may seem, on the surface, more academic than useful is *whether the flow of information is controlled by the sender or by the receiver*. In television and radio the information flow is entirely in the hands of the sender, whereas in print media the receiver determines the pace at which he takes in information, the order in which he accepts the elements and the relative time he spends with each.

This characteristic of television and radio can be useful when you're advertising a product to someone who thinks he doesn't need it or to someone in the family who doesn't normally make that product decision and might flip past a print ad. For example, a woman generally is not interested in automotive batteries despite the fact that as a frequent driver she relies on their dependability. But by setting up a problem situation she can recognize as her own, then presenting the DieHard battery as the solution, television or radio advertising can interest her in the product. This is one of broadcast's great strengths for the advertiser.

Because the viewer doesn't know what's coming next, broadcast provides an opportunity to surprise, to pull a switch, to present the product or its benefit in a context of the unexpected, thus contributing to memorability. This characteristic is part of what makes television the ideal medium for demonstration. But the information-flow advantages are not all on the side of broadcast. Putting the control in the hands of the receiver permits him to go back and reread something that particularly interested him, to cut out a coupon, or a recipe or—that greatest compliment of all to the advertising person—to tear out the entire ad.

Related to control of information flow but somewhat different is *control of informational quantity.* Although longer spots are possible when advertisers, such as Hallmark, buy an entire program, sixty seconds is the maximum length available to most television advertisers and thirty seconds is the norm. This means that usually only one point can be made and the supportive information is severely limited. In print, the amount of information is theoretically unlimited. Type and graphics can be crammed into the page to the limits of the reader's assumed interest and visual powers. Additional pages can be purchased to the limits of the client's budget. Voluminous information can be transmitted. Obviously, magazines and newspapers are better media for products about which consumers demand a lot of facts before purchase, but television is unexcelled at achieving fast and broad awareness of a product and its primary benefit. So we're beginning to see the advantages of the "media mix."

Linked closely to the amount of information a medium can transmit for the advertiser are *the conditions under which that information and the intended recipient normally meet.* Magazines and newspapers receive the most intense and uninterrupted concentration of attention from the reader, and we can assume that a similar degree of attention goes into any advertisement the reader chooses to enter. This is friendly territory for advertising: a magazine ad is at least benignly tolerated, often warmly welcomed; newspaper studies consistently show advertising as an important reason for purchasing the paper. Not necessarily so with outdoor, which provides no sugarcoating for the message other than what it can develop for itself.

Radio usually reaches its listener while he's doing something else: driving, washing dishes, studying, working, etc. The message must separate itself from the program material and command a different level of attention, but not in such a way as to be inappropriate for the audience, which has chosen that station for its consistent character.

No one is certain, as yet, exactly how a person interacts with television. He is "viewing," but we can't be sure he's watching and listening. The attention is of a different nature, if not at a lower level, than that devoted to a magazine page. The mind is in a less inquisitive, less acquisitive state. At any rate, the commercial represents an intrusion. The mind begins to shift gears. What degree and variety of attention, if any, is directed at the commercial depends on what happens in the first five seconds.

Color is a somewhat more objective consideration. The importance of color varies in each advertising situation, and the quality of color varies with each medium. Magazines provide the best and truest color, newspapers the poorest. But then, color should be used for different purposes in each. Newspaper color can seldom convey appetite appeal; that is the realm of magazines. On the other hand, a red headline will not stand out in a magazine the way it will on a newspaper page. Color in outdoor is tricky and can't be relied on for delicate jobs. After several weeks of brutal sun, reds can turn to pinks, skin tones can go pale. Television color, from the transmitter, is second only to magazine color. What happens to it when it's translated into dots on the individual screen of each differently adjusted set is another matter. Since we can do nothing about this, we use color in commercials with an average set in mind and pray. Some say that radio provides the truest color, but it all rests on the abilities of the creative group. Since the picture is assembled in the listener's mind, the words and sounds used to evoke color determine its hue, chroma and clarity.

A final consideration is what we call *editorial environment*—the suitability of each medium to the specific product and message, what the surroundings will add to or subtract from the effectiveness of the advertisement. Assessing this factor depends on the experience, sensitivity and judgment of the professional media planner and his current familiarity with each magazine, newspaper and program vehicle under consideration. A computer might assign similar values to *New York* magazine and the *New Yorker*. The media planner on the Bermuda Tourism account might give them quite different weights on the basis of editorial environment.

Finding the right balance among these eight considerations calls for a logical, analytical mind. Still, there is ample opportunity for creativity, for the unexpected. Several years ago, our media planners in Los Angeles saw an opportunity to fulfill all the statistical demands of the Sunkist lemon program by placing the entire budget in one magazine. The result, with as many as three spreads running in a single issue, was a dramatic increase in impact.

At this point the media planner has determined which media type or types might be best suited for the job. Now these qualitative judgments must be synchronized with the mountains of numbers he has assembled. The media themselves and the specialized research companies can provide us with the number of people likely to be exposed to the message if it appeared in any newspaper or magazine or was broadcast on any program of any station or network. For budgeting purposes, this number is usually expressed as cost per thousand readers or viewers.

Since logic dictates that not all those people will actually receive the message as opposed to just being somewhere in the vicinity when it's delivered, we assign numerical weights to each possible media choice on the basis of qualitative considerations. Doing this in two stages, we first arrive at the probable audience for our message rather than the remotely possible, and we then gauge the ability of our message to really involve, interest and convince our prospect in the specific context of a particular magazine or program. This gives us the cost per thousand real dialogues with real prospects, a much more useful number.

We now have a pretty good idea of what our "reach" should be—the prospects to whom we must present our message and the manner in which we'll do so. The next step is to determine how many times we have to deliver the message to each prospect in order to have it considered. As any parent, boss, suitor or salesman knows, asking once is not enough. This factor is known as "frequency," and the determination of adequate frequency depends upon the media, the kind of prospect, and primarily the kind of product and how often the prospect might usually be in the market for such a purchase.

Once the media plan is complete and has been approved by the client, the buyers go to work actually contracting for the space and time. A lot of negotiating, sometimes haggling, goes on here. And finally there is the follow-through. Someone must verify that every ad and spot actually ran when and where it was supposed to, and in the form intended. Discrepancies result in further negotiating and haggling. In the end, the agency pays the media for the space and time delivered—and when everything is working right, the client pays the agency at about the same time. The difference in the two payments is 15%, which covers everything we've described thus far, the research we're about to discuss, and my salary.

RESEARCH

Up to this point we've been following the development process of an advertisement more or less chronologically. But research has played a vital part throughout, even in media analysis. Research provides the stuff that ads are made of: information. Thus it is the most important function of all. Without research the campaign would be without compass and rudder. Without it an advertisement would be empty.

Research in its broadest sense is also our point of contact with the consumer, our lifeline to reality. It is essential, then, that the information coming in through this conduit be complete, be accurate and be interpreted by people with an understanding of the true nature of advertising and its implicit contract with the consumer.

Research divides neatly into four functional and sequential stages: market definition, creative development, pre-testing and tracking. Concentrating on any one phase to the exclusion of the others is usually hazardous, but if such concentration is unavoidable, it should be on the two earlier stages. That's when consumer attitudes and opinions can do most to shape the strategy and influence the idea and execution.

Market definition takes place before a writer or art director ever puts pencil to paper. Indeed, without some form of it, that pencil will probably be moving in the wrong direction. Market definition sets out to answer questions about the persons, the individuals, who will be the most promising prospects for our product, questions about the competition our product faces in the broad reality of their lives, questions about what must be communicated to them in order to get their interest, their assent, their mental commitment to find, buy and try the product.

163

These are similar to the questions that have to be answered by the strategy; and strategy development is the purpose of this stage of research.

The first step in market definition is what we call desk research. This is simply the accumulation of all existing data about the product category, the company, the product itself and the competition—and, most important, the information necessary to define and understand the consumer. Desk research requires a good detective to dig up all pertinent material buried in the files and minds of people in the client company. It requires a good librarian to search out the gems scattered through industry studies, previous advertising research, government sources and such treasure troves as the *Yankelovich Monitor, How the Consumer Feels* and *Roper Reports*. And it requires a dedicated analyst to sort it all out, digest it and write a brief that puts it in an organized, synthesized and useful package.

The second step is filling any important gaps revealed by the desk research. This can mean anything from a relatively simple study of consumer attitudes about the product (why users buy it, why nonusers don't, why previous users rejected it) to ambitious segmentation research in which prospects are categorized into life-style or attitudinal groups in order to link their characteristics with attributes of the product and thus define consumer "need groups." Exploratory studies might also be undertaken at this point to get a better feel for the consumer in relation to the product, to get a clearer understanding of where it fits into his or her life, to hear consumers speak and see their reactions. It's important that the people who will be making the advertising and evolving the strategy be physically present at these sessions. They must see and hear how real people respond to questions about the product.

The final step of market definition is often an evaluation of possible selling propositions that begin to emerge from the information. Selling propositions are merely the various benefits of the product measured against one another for their relative importance and exclusivity. Usually they're put in the form of simple posters: a picture and a headline. Because respondents understandably desire to appear practical and prudent to the interviewer, the problem with most proposition screening is that it tends to give an inordinate advantage to price benefits and a disadvantage to emotional ones. But if the basic information is good and adequate, the most promising benefit will be apparent by this time.

Creative development research normally begins after the strategy has been agreed upon and, as the name implies, guides the stage during which various creative executions are conceived, worked out and exposed to prototypical prospects. Its purpose is to make certain, through consumer exposure and a reading of the response, that the recipient of the communication ultimately perceives exactly what we intend for him to perceive. We might want to know what people really understand after seeing a photograph or reading certain words or headlines, how they feel about an actor or actress we might be considering as a spokesperson, or how they respond to a piece of music.

The techniques are simple and usually inexpensive, involving groups of consumers and a professional moderator. But it's also important that the agency people listen in. Consumer viewpoints, wording, nuances of language, can often suggest executional approaches or shape copy style. We've found time and again that great headlines often drop from the lips of housewives. Very frankly, that's where I got the headline "Loaded with soap" for S.O.S. Soap Pads years ago. Talking with consumers on the telephone is also very helpful at this stage.

This kind of grass-roots research helps develop hunches and insights that we might then want to verify on a larger and more national scale. We employ a number of techniques for this, including, for simpler tasks, our program that gives us fast access to a national sample of 1,500 men and women who in income, age, education and location represent a mini-America.

Sometimes we merely ask respondents to play back what they've gleaned from reading headlines, copy or rough layouts, or from listening to sample sound tracks. Other times we employ the tachistoscope, a machine that limits the respondent's viewing time so we can determine what an element or layout

JOHN O'TOOLE

communicates at a glance. Or we may use a variation on this technique that allows the respondent to see the ad again if he chooses and for as long as he chooses. This indicates the ad's ability to stop the prospect on the page.

There are a wide variety of tools because research at this stage is flexible and can be adapted to various jobs and various kinds of information needs. And this stage is important, because the earlier research is begun, the more likely we are to be heading in the right direction.

Pre-testing takes place after a concept has been executed to the point of a comprehensive layout or a television storyboard. At any rate, this is the least expensive way. There are times when an idea simply cannot be adequately communicated without a finished photograph or optics or music.

Because it occurs so late in the process and there is so much riding on the results, pre-testing is the most controversial of the four research stages. Its purpose is to determine, before making large media expenditures, whether the ad or commercial gets the prospect's attention, fulfills the strategy and communicates its points in a convincing, persuasive manner. And, equally important, if it doesn't, why not?

Pre-testing is a useful tool. Misused it can be worse than useless; it can be misleading. It is misused when it becomes the sole basis on which an ad or commercial is judged. And it is misused when deductions made from commercials that have tested well are allowed to dictate rigid formats to which all future commercials must be written. The fact that so many television commercials today fall into formats results, I suspect, from this kind of misuse. Copywriters, canny creatures that they are, know what the testing systems can and cannot measure. And if their work is going to be judged solely on the basis of a test, they can easily learn to write to formats that are really artifacts of that test and its limitations.

Despite its great popularity, pre-testing is not a predictor of what will happen in the marketplace. Too many other factors influence sales. Nor will testing a single ad or commercial measure the effects of a whole campaign, with its multiple exposure and variations of execution. What pre-testing can provide is some idea of the attention-getting value of a proposed ad or commercial. But since attention, as every child knows, can be gained in a number of annoying or rude ways, pre-testing cannot replace a devotion to the implicit contract. It can measure what is and isn't being communicated and generally how persuasive the message is—but only in relationship to other ads and commercials that are being tested at the same time or have been tested in the past. Testing well on those attributes increases your chance of being successful but does not a sale make.

For pre-testing television commercials, there are three major kinds of services: on-air testing, in-theater testing and forced-exposure testing. On-air testing involves telephoning to find and question people who have actually been exposed to the commercial in their own living rooms the preceding night. It's a way of determining how many people were sufficiently impressed to remember having seen the commercial among a barrage of other messages and discovering what they learned from it. But the number of respondents is usually small. Furthermore, you can achieve memorability simply by having the presenter drop his pants or including a dog that barks "The Star Spangled Banner."

A more serious problem is that certain kinds of commercials always fare badly in day-after recall tests. And they're often the ones advertising agency people consider most effective as well as most popular with consumers: commercials based on emotion rather than logic, on visual and musical communication rather than merely verbal. Day-after recall methods require respondents to verbalize their recollection of the message, and people find this very difficult to do with a commercial that's primarily emotional or nonverbal in nature. But it's easy with a highly logical, linear commercial in which all the verbalization has been done for them—and probably redone several times.

FCB proved this in 1981 by devising a new way to determine if people could recall a commercial. The method was called "masked recognition." we simply masked out the product in the picture and bleeped out any reference to it in the sound. We showed these masked commercials to people who had been exposed to the unmasked versions the previous night, asked them to identify the product, then compared our results with those of day-after recall testing of the same commercials. While the scores of logical, verbal commercials improved 19% by the new method, the scores of emotional commercials went up 68%.

In-theater testing brings about 200 people into a theater to see pilot films of television shows as well as pilot commercials. It generally uses roughly produced commercials rather than the expensive finished commercials shown on the air. It involves larger samples than any on-air testing system. But 200 people sitting together in a darkened theater with their eyes riveted to a large screen is hardly a normal television viewing situation.

In the forced-exposure techniques, people are brought together in small groups and asked to pay attention to a commercial. They're told they will be asked questions about it. No attempt is made to simulate a program environment. Forced exposure generates good information about what viewers did and did not get out of the message, but it obviously gives very little indication of attention-getting value.

Pre-testing of print ads is generally done by inserting test ads into a magazine or portfolio of test and control ads. People are asked to look through the magazine or portfolio at their own pace; they are questioned, then asked to go back and discuss ads in more detail.

Whether it's for an ad or a commercial, pre-testing can be helpful in the context of a total program of research. Because of what it can and cannot measure, it will not always screen out flaws. Being short-term in nature, pre-testing will not generally eliminate advertising that, over time, annoys or insults consumers.

Tracking is the research tool that comes closest to really measuring the effect of advertising because it isolates and studies the effects of the entire communications program in the marketplace.

Tracking requires clearly defined objectives for the communications. What level of awareness do we want to attain among legitimate prospects for the product or service? What level of purchase intent? What attitudes do we want to affect and to what degree? In what period of time do we want to accomplish

168

what? The procedure is to do a "benchmark" study before the advertising runs, then to do periodic tracking studies that measure awareness and attitude changes through time.

Besides giving the client some degree of confidence that his money is being prudently invested, tracking provides valuable information to help make the advertising more effective. If awareness isn't increasing rapidly enough, if certain attitudes or intentions are not changing according to strategy, if unforeseen outside influences are creating new imperatives, the execution can be adjusted during the course of the campaign or the strategy can be altered.

These four stages of research represent the ideal program. In my experience, the most successful advertising results, over the long haul, from this kind of thorough information gathering. But it's not always possible. There is a limit to the research budgets of most clients. Given this reality, the place to concentrate limited research dollars or facilities is up front. The earlier information is used to develop strategy and guide the creation of advertising, the fewer the possibilities for error and the greater the chances for success.

Be it a minimum or maximum program, it's important for advertising people to keep in mind that research is not a substitute for judgment but, properly used, an indispensable source of sustenance and guidance. At its best, it's like having the prospect himself sitting beside you advising you what's important and what isn't, what's believable and what isn't, what's appropriate and what isn't, what's insulting to his intelligence and what isn't. But just as we wouldn't expect the prospect to actually write our ad or commercial for us, we shouldn't let the research do it.

PART IV

*Aspects
and
varieties
of the
species*

AGENCIES

The advertising agency is one of those simple American inventions that, to the consternation of some and the benefit of many, has succeeded beyond the dreams of its originators and taken up residence everywhere in the free world.

The oldest agency still in existence is J. Walter Thompson, founded in 1864. Next comes N. W. Ayer, which was founded in Philadelphia in 1869. The third oldest is Albert Frank–Guenther Law, founded in New York in 1872 and, curiously enough, acquired by Foote, Cone & Belding, the fourth oldest, in 1978. Foote, Cone & Belding, as you know, was born in Chicago in 1873 under the name Lord & Thomas.

No one really knows how many advertising agencies there are. We do know that more than 500 belong to the American Association of Advertising Agencies, and that accounts for all the large ones except for that perpetual nonconformist Jerry della Femina and his Della Femina, Travisano & Partners, which ranks about thirty-fifth in dollar volume. The Standard Directory of Advertising Agencies lists almost 3,000 that are willing to state their yearly billings; about 2,400 bill less than $5,000,000. When I moved from Los Angeles in 1967, I counted 250 listings under "Advertising Agencies" in just the Los Angeles and Orange Counties classified directories.

A graph of all these agencies in terms of dollar volume would look like a worm with its head raised. The head would represent the twenty that do almost two-thirds of all the advertising in the United States. Towards the tail you would find many one- or two-person shops struggling to make a living on a couple of local retail accounts. At the tip of the nose would be Young & Rubicam with more than 6,000 employees in 120 offices, and

173

J. Walter Thompson Co. with a staff of more than 7,000 people in 100 offices.

Of the 51,000 people in those 500 AAAA agencies, two-thirds of them work in just five cities—New York, Chicago, Detroit, Los Angeles and San Francisco—and 43% work in New York, where slightly less than half of all advertising is done. In the larger agencies, they generally do one of four things: they are in account management, which means they coordinate and supervise the services of the agency for the particular advertiser to which they are assigned; or they're in the creative department, writing, designing, filming or otherwise contributing to the actual preparation of advertisements; or they're in media, planning or buying space and time; or they're in research, gathering and interpreting the information without which the others could not do their jobs. That's a flagrant oversimplification, of course, but essentially accurate.

These four functions are most often the organizational basis of any agency; the other jobs in a large agency—management, for example—are of far less importance. Individuals from each of the four departments work on a client's advertising business as part of an "account team." Almost everyone works in more than one account team, a practice that provides people with refreshing variety and makes more efficient use of their time.

And time is the commodity with which an agency's management deals. Careful records must be kept of the hours each individual devotes to any client every day. Only by converting those hours to what they cost the agency and comparing the cost to what we receive from the client can we determine how much money we're making—or losing. Only by making those hours more productive—by hiring, inspiring, caring for and combining the right people—can we surpass our competitors.

So it's a very simple business, the advertising agency business, as well as a small one. The visibility of its product and the importance of it to this mercantile society are out of all proportion to its size and the number of workers involved.

Each agency, at least among the larger ones, does pretty much the same sorts of things pretty much the same way. A visitor would see few differences other than the physical surroundings. Even prospective clients interviewing a number of agencies often have difficulty discovering meaningful differences in approach and make their decisions on the basis of the individuals who would be assigned to their account team.

Nor is there as much difference as the uninitiated might expect in the style of advertising produced by each agency. There is no identifiable look or single approach that characterizes any of the leading agencies. There couldn't be, because they work in such a variety of categories—from bar soap to bubble gum to brokerage houses—that no uniform style could be maintained. Furthermore, most important advertisers employ scores of marketing experts who exert no little influence on the appearance and content of the advertising for which they're paying. An advertising agency is more like an architect—considering the specific purpose of the building and the needs of its inhabitants and the tastes of the builder—than it is like a poet.

Nevertheless there are differences among the large agencies, some organizational or directional, some philosophical. And these can have an effect on the advertising they tend to produce, which in turn can have an effect on the way consumers perceive advertising in general. They can also have an effect on the working environment, which influences how happy an individual will be at any particular agency. These differences are more apparent, and more important, to those of us who spend our days in the agency business than to others. Still, I'll point them out for readers with a taste for this sort of esoterica.

The biggest American advertising agency is Young & Rubicam. (I am assigning rankings here in terms of total worldwide income as reported for 1980 by *Advertising Age* rather than in terms of volume in the United States. The distinction is more than academic, as you will see later, but not in this case: Y&R is number one in both categories.) Young & Rubicam was founded in 1923 by John Orr Young and Raymond Rubicam. Despite its surging into first place ahead of J. Walter Thompson in 1980, Y&R is regarded less for its size than for its ability to produce very high quality advertising. Its commercials for Jello-O are a good example.

I asked Ed Ney, chairman of Y&R, to define the essential difference between his agency and the rest. He said,

> Our credo is to "understand through discipline and compel through imagination." By this I mean that Y&R attempts to understand what forces lead to compelling communications so that we can develop the right strategy, make the product a hero, make the communication believable, create drama, make a friend of the consumer, and build a long-term personality for the brand or service.

If all that is somewhat reminiscent of ideals put forth in earlier sections of this book, it is not a result of collusion. I was startled by the similarity myself. A partial explanation may lie in the fact that Young was trained at Lord & Thomas. I prefer to think of it as corroboration. And as another explanation for my longtime admiration for Y&R. This admiration was undiminished, perhaps even strengthened, by the reputation Y&R had for several recent years as an agency that worked its people very hard. It is said that a sign once appeared in the creative department at Y&R/New York that read, "If you don't show up on Saturday, don't bother coming in Sunday."

Second to Y&R by a nose is J. Walter Thompson Co. In fact, had it not formed the JWT Group in 1980, of which J. Walter Thompson Co. is just a part, and had it reported its total income as a single agency, it would still be in the top spot. For Thompson is big. Even though it was passed by Y&R on a technicality, it is still thought of by most of us as the big U.S. agency. And it is everywhere, having followed its giant multinational American clients into the most remote corners of the globe—clients such as Ford and Kodak. Its present chief, Don Johnston, was previously in charge of the overseas units.

It may come as a surprise to some that Don Johnston and other agency heads to whom I refer are my friends. The agency business is generally and accurately regarded as highly competitive. But like most competitive activities, it engenders a mutual respect and a bond among those in the fray. We enjoy one another. Some of us play tennis together. Those who still go in for sports that involve striking a ball in repose play golf together.

McCann-Erickson, seventy years old, ranks third among U.S.-based agencies on a worldwide basis but fourteenth in terms of the United States alone. This is a result of the agency's early expansion overseas and the enormous volume of advertising done abroad by its American clients, among them Coca-Cola and General Motors. While the mention of Coke brings to mind some of the outstanding commercials of the decade ("I'd like to buy the world a Coke" and "Mean Joe Green"), and while McCann strives for quality, its overseas business is so dominant that it shapes the agency's identity. Within the business, we think of McCann-Erickson primarily as the agency upon which the sun never sets. It, too, is currently headed by the ex-chief of its non-U.S. division, the genial Gene Kummel.

Gene provided me with this encapsulation of what characterizes McCann advertising:

> We like to think that at McCann-Erickson we produce advertising that sells . . . from a system that works. But what starts the sale—whether it's a packet of margarine or a supermarket, an automobile, a soft drink or a cup of coffee—is a common approach or *attitude*.
>
> We believe advertising has to do with creating relevant relationships between people and products. *We must place our product in people's lives.* Anyone who gets that right—doesn't go far wrong.

Number 4 in the world and number 3 in the United States is Ogilvy & Mather, founded as Hewitt, Ogilvy, Benson & Mather in 1948 by one of the most colorful, successful and respected individuals in our business, David Ogilvy. David was born in England. After working as a chef in a Paris hotel and as a stove salesman in Scotland, he moved to these shores and went to work for George Gallup's Audience Research Institute. But he was destined to be a copywriter. As evidence of how quickly and grandly his agency burgeoned, it is the most recently founded among the top ten. It is also the only one of that group in which the guiding genius of one man is so pervasive that the agency can be referred to as "his," even though David has moved to his chateau outside Paris and now functions as the keeper of creative standards. Jock Elliott, his longtime associate, is chairman; early in 1981, he turned the chief executive function over to the president, Bill Phillips.

Jock describes Ogilvy & Mather as

> the agency spawned by David Ogilvy, with his un-compromising standards of creative brilliance, good taste and dedication to the basic principles of selling. A cadre of gentlemen, and gentlewomen, with brains. A company devoted to J. P. Morgan's precept, "Only first-class business, and that in a first-class way."

David himself has written volumes on the subject of advertising, one of which, *Confessions of an Advertising Man*, pretty well defines the standards Jock mentioned.

I think most of us in the craft would agree that David and his agency have demonstrated an unusual respect for the consumer's intelligence in their work. From the early "Man in the Hathaway Shirt" campaign and the famous Rolls-Royce ad, "At 60 miles an hour, the loudest noise in the new Rolls-Royce comes from the electric clock," to the current campaigns for American Express, the prospect never feels he's being talked down to. As David once wrote, "The consumer is not an idiot. She is your wife." Nevertheless, O&M was responsible some years ago for the doves that were continually flying into women's kitchens and the crowns that magically appeared on people's heads when they tasted Imperial Margarine.

Number 5 around the world and sixth in the United States is Ted Bates & Co., founded in 1940. It is now run by Bob Jacoby, short in stature and long on competitiveness. Describing the agency, Bob says,

Ted Bates differs from other agencies in its strict adherence to the U.S.P. (Unique Selling Proposition) disciplines, which demand the discovery of a unique or preemptive consumer benefit before advertising executions are created. It matters not whether the execution is clinical, emotional or imagery, a precise benefit of importance will emerge from *every* Bates advertisement.

The agency's adherence to this philosophy was for a long while combined with a disregard for the sense and sensibility of the consumer. The result was a style of advertising that irritated some while selling many. A lot of us tagged Bates as the "Fast, fast, fast relief" and "hammers-in-the-head" agency. During that period they tore a lot of rents in the fabric of the implicit contract.

But the same philosophy can guide strategy in a way that produces commercials the prospect will welcome and even enjoy. And this has been happening at Bates over the past several years. I suspect Bob Jacoby, who took the reins in 1973, changed course in that direction. The "Taste the high country" campaign for Coors beer and "A piece of The Rock" for Prudential would not have come out of the old Ted Bates agency.

Number 6 in worldwide ranking and seventh in the United States is BBDO. The well-known initials stand for Batten, Barton, Durstine and Osborn—which Fred Allen once said sounded like a trunk falling down the stairs. BBDO was founded in 1891 and leapt to the top ranks in 1948 when it acquired the Lucky Strike account, which Foote, Cone & Belding had resigned. It is run by Bruce Crawford now that the universally loved and puckish Tom Dillon has retired. Bruce is a capable executive who, following what seems to be an emerging pattern, earned his spurs on the international side.

My first job was at BBDO in Chicago, where the copy chief, Gordon White, now a professor at the University of Illinois, seemed to be the only person in advertising willing to give a poet a crack at copy. So there remains a warm spot in my heart

179

for this agency, despite the memory I and other alumni retain of a certain penury on the part of the management. BBDO was the only agency in town that made its employees punch in and out on a time card. Once I neglected to do so and was taken to task by my boss. The next day another copywriter tacked this verse to my wall:

> For it's B and it's B and it's D and it's O,
> And don't ever forget to punch in, John,
> Or out when you go
> Lest BBD and O
> Become merely a place where you've been, John.

Doggerel has always been abundant in advertising agency corridors. At BBDO a fellow writer once showed me a book of limericks, one for every major agency then in business. The only one I can recall immortalized an agency of which little has been heard in recent years, perhaps for reasons suggested by the poet:

> The ladies at Lambert & Feasly
> All fornicate freely and easily.
> They do it, they say,
> To augment the pay
> Which at Lambert & Feasly is measly.

The BBDO approach begins with positioning that establishes the brand as the solution to a particular problem the consumer has, using the most competitive balance of product performance, emotion and price. This approach has produced highly effective and highly regarded campaigns for such clients as Campbell's Soup and Pepsi Cola—but from the same people came "Ring Around the Collar" for Wisk. Obviously some consideration beyond those included in our creative credos is needed to keep all of us within the bounds of our implicit contract with the consumer.

Number 7 worldwide and fifth-ranked in the United States is the Leo Burnett Company, founded in Chicago in 1935. Since this was the depths of the Depression, Leo always kept a bowl of apples in his reception area to remind himself and others what they'd be selling if they weren't successful at selling advertising. Leo, a squat, homely, single-minded advertising genius, died in 1971, but the apples remain. So does his legacy, a determination to base every campaign on "the inherent drama" that is to be found in every product. The campaigns of this agency are, to an unusual degree, admired by those of us in the business and liked by those without. They include Kellogg cereals, Marlboro cigarettes, Charlie the Tuna, Green Giant and Allstate Insurance.

The current head of Leo Burnett Co. is Jack Kopp, who defines the agency's approach this way:

> Burnett advertising makes two appeals at the same time. The first is to the head. It seeks to inform the consumer of those practical and sensible virtues of the product. This is important because it talks directly to the consumer's *needs*.
>
> The second appeal is to the heart. It seeks to involve the consumer in a fundamental appeal that touches him personally. It looks for that emotional "high ground" that transcends the product. It is even more vital than the first appeal, because it talks directly to the consumer's *wants*.
>
> Burnett advertising has just a little more heart than head.

Burnett is unusual in having only one U.S. operation, a giant office in Chicago. All its work for all its domestic clients, no matter where they're located, is done in Chicago. Indeed, until the company bought the big London Press Exchange in 1969 and became a major international agency, the Chicago headquarters was its only advertising office anywhere in the world. Leo used to make a point of this, saying that Midwest simplicity and what he called the "sodbuster" mentality resulted in advertising that was closer to the consumer.

SSC&B, founded in 1946 as Sullivan, Stauffer, Colwell & Bayles, is ranked number 8 in terms of its worldwide volume, but it is only twenty-eighth in the United States. This anomaly is due to the SSC&B acquisition of 49% of Lintas, the giant agency that operates just about everywhere in the world except America (Unilever retained 51% of Lintas—which stands for Lever International Advertising Service). SSC&B is thought of in association with its advertising for such products as Lipton Iced Tea Mix, Johnson's Baby Shampoo and Cover Girl Cosmetics: professional work for big packaged-goods advertisers. The agency is led today by the statesmanlike Al Seaman.

A word should be added here about mergers, for SSC&B was involved in the biggest acquisition in advertising history. It was bought in 1979 by Interpublic, a colossal holding company that owns McCann-Erickson as well, to say nothing of Campbell-Ewald (number 14) and Marschalk (number 33). Ogilvy & Mather owns Scali, McCabe & Sloves (number 31); Young & Rubicam owns Marsteller, Inc. (number 19); BBDO owns Doremus (number 39); Ted Bates owns Campbell-Mithum (number 28). Foote, Cone & Belding acquired Honig, Cooper & Harrington, the largest agency in the West, in 1975, Aitkin-Kynett in 1977 and Albert Frank–Guenther Law in 1978. This is just a partial list and completely ignores the many specialized agencies that have been acquired by the larger consumer-products agencies. It also ignores the even greater number of overseas agencies that have been bought, wholly or partially, by the same big U.S. agencies. More about both later.

Clearly mergers and acquisitions have been the predominant characteristic of the agency business as a whole since the end of the sixties. There are many reasons: the economies of scale, the desire of principals to get their money out, the growing complexity and expense of serving sophisticated clients. But the result is that the big agencies are getting bigger, small ones continue to be spawned each year, and the middle-sized are diminishing in number.

The ninth largest agency on a worldwide basis is Foote, Cone & Belding. However, it is the fourth largest in the United States. The disparity is a result of our having started on the international path later than most of our competitors. We're catching up pretty quickly, though.

Probably enough has been said about FCB in these pages for

you to glean an impression of its essential character. All I need add is that organizationally FCB is the opposite of Leo Burnett. Our offices are in many marketing centers and function as complete, full-service agencies. Thus, rather than one huge office operating alone or with branches, FCB has four agencies of about the same size in four different U.S. cities. Similarly, it has its corporate officers spread across the country rather than concentrated in one location. As Foote and Cone and Belding resided in New York, Chicago and Los Angeles respectively, so did the succeeding management of O'Toole, Art Schultz and Lou Scott.

Number 10 worldwide and thirteenth in the United States is D'Arcy-MacManus & Masius. This agency is the product of a 1971 merger between two U.S. agencies, D'Arcy and MacManus–John & Adams, and then of a partnership formed in 1973 with Masius, a major U.K. agency that had offices throughout Europe, Australia, New Zealand and South Africa. Because of this synthesizing of identities, it is difficult for most of us in the business to form, at this point, a sharp impression of D'Arcy-MacManus or to define its dominant characteristic. Indeed, that may be its dominant characteristic.

But to Jim Orthwein, the agency's chairman, the essential difference is a system they call Belief Dynamics. He explains it this way:

> All behavior is based on beliefs and feelings. To change behavior you must create, alter or intensify certain beliefs. It's advertising's job to encounter and alter an existing belief system in a way that will lead to the behavior the client is paying us to have occur.

I'm not certain exactly how this approach works in practice or how close it would be to those of other agencies when stripped of the jargon. But if it has had anything to do with the fine advertising D'Arcy-MacManus has consistently done for Budweiser and Michelob beers, there must be something to it.

Doyle Dane Bernbach is eleventh in world ranking and number 8 in the United States. This is an agency with a very sharp

183

identity, due to the brilliance and diligence of Bill Bernbach, who, along with Max Dane and Ned Doyle, founded the business in 1949. DDB is not only associated in the industry with certain of its current clients (Volkswagen, Polaroid Land Cameras), but, on the strength of past campaigns, with clients they no longer have ("We're #2. So we try harder" for Avis and "What a spicy meatball" for Alka-Seltzer).

I asked Bill Bernbach to give me four or five sentences that described the essential difference in his agency. He told me that not even the most skillful *Reader's Digest* editor could do that. So I dipped into some of the things Bill has written—anyone who cares about this business keeps everything Bill Bernbach writes—and strung the recurring themes together into this statement:

> We don't stop after marketing and research have told us *what* to say. We make them pay off with *how* we say it. Advertising is fundamentally persuasion, and persuasion happens to be not a science but an art.
>
> The most criminal waste of money in business today is that spent on advertising that never gets looked at. Properly practiced, creativity can lift your claims out of the swamp of sameness and make them accepted, believed, persuasive, urgent.

In practicing those beliefs on behalf of its clients, Doyle Dane Bernbach has done a great deal to strengthen the consumer's faith in the implicit contract.

Number 12 worldwide and ninth in the United States is Grey Advertising. Grey is another one that's hard to get a handle on, even though it's been in business since 1917. In its early years, Grey was known as a retail and garment industry agency. Its client list now, however, includes many major brands from such marketing giants as Procter & Gamble, General Foods, Gillette and Revlon. Yet few campaigns spring to mind when the name Grey is mentioned.

Under the leadership of Ed Meyer, the agency has grown rapidly in recent years and expanded into many new markets in the United States and abroad. Ed attributes this success to a concept called Brand Character™. "Simply put," Ed says,

> this trademarked concept is the combined perception of the product as a "what" (the brand itself and its strategic positioning) and a "who" (the emotional response to its individuality). Properly developed, Brand Character™ becomes the springboard for the creative leap that sets a brand apart from all others in a single category, identifies it, and personalizes it in a way that is distinctive, appealing and enduring.

That makes an even dozen of the top agencies and provides an appropriate number at which to stop and consider their real role in affecting public attitudes about advertising in general. Those twelve agencies, while differing widely in character and organization, while stating their beliefs about the craft in their own vocabularies, share a general perception of what constitutes effective advertising that will also be welcomed by consumers. I'm convinced that if the creative directors of all twelve were brought into a room and asked to evaluate an evening's worth of commercials on that basis, there would be virtual unanimity about what's good and what isn't. Furthermore, they all want to do only the former and, within the trade, to have their own and their agencies' names associated with it. Still, each of those agencies has on occasion violated the implicit contract. Some more than others. Some inadvertently, some deliberately. Why?

The influence an agency has over the quality of a client's advertising is vast but not final. Most clients, too, want advertising that is both effective and welcome, but their interpretations of what is permitted by the implicit contract vary widely. And sometimes what the client finds acceptable is something the agency—and you or I—would deem unacceptable. If the client is unyielding, he will eventually get what he wants, either by introducing gradual changes that alter the character of the work or by demanding or by going to another agency. These instances are rare. So, too, are flagrant violations by agencies of the size we've been talking about—rare but destructive.

The only way to avoid them is for an agency to have a set of beliefs about advertising and its obligation to the consumer that go beyond a creative philosophy or procedure, to be persuasive about them when arguing such issues with a client and have the courage to resign when the differences are irreconcilable. Strong medicine, the latter, and not often necessary. For clients, as we're about to discover, are generally pretty reasonable and likable people. Particularly those who pay their bills on time.

CLIENTS

A client is an advertiser as seen through the eyes of an advertising agency. A prospect is someone else's client.

The term "client" can refer to the company with whom the agency deals or to any of the individuals within it, from chairman to assistant brand manager. Either way, there is no greater force in the battle for advertising that fulfills both sales objectives and consumer expectations than a smart, sensitive, courageous client who believes in advertising because he has experienced its awesome power.

Far and away the biggest national advertiser in America is the Procter & Gamble Company. In 1979, P&G spent $615 million to advertise and promote its many brands. Sears, Roebuck and Co. actually spent more, but half its budget was for local advertising. As a national advertiser, Sears was third with $379 million. General Foods was well behind P&G, having spent $393 million on its long list of brands. General Motors was fourth at $323 million, and Philip Morris, Inc. fifth with $291 million. All in all, the 100 leading national advertisers spent a total of $11.7 billion dollars in 1979. They did not spend that enormous sum because they were looking for a way to get rid of it. They spent it because advertising works and there is nothing else that can produce the same results.

Looking over the list of top advertisers, one is struck by the success and stature of the companies. It's also interesting to note how many companies that are part of the advertising process themselves employ it heavily to benefit their own businesses. RCA, CBS, Time Inc., Warner Communications and ABC are all on that exclusive roster. The closer you are to it, the more you believe in it. Another revealing item on the list is that the twenty-eighth largest national advertiser in America—obviously convinced of the value and unique role of advertising—is the United States Government.

Now, any expenditure measured in billions is bound to raise eyebrows and attract scrutiny (unless, that is, it's spent by the twenty-eighth largest advertiser). But some facts are needed to put the figures in perspective. One is that advertising adds just pennies, sometimes mils, to the cost of most products you buy. And without the economies of mass production made possible by mass marketing made possible by advertising, many products we take for granted would be out of reach for the average person.

Also significant is the fact that over the long term, the total expenditure for advertising in America has not grown at all as a percentage of the gross national product. It is no greater today than it was in 1925. In addition, the public gets free television and radio programming and cheap magazines and newspapers. Few of us could pay what would have to be charged per program or per issue if advertisers were not supporting these media. Or we would pay with our taxes, thus giving government total control over everything we see, hear and read.

So advertisers are not such bad fellows, particularly when they're trying hard to make their messages live up to the terms of the implicit contract. And most of them are. That does not mean, however, that they aren't sometimes frustrating.

I was once presenting some ideas for a television commercial to the marketing director of the Kimberly-Clark Corporation, a man not known for his cheery disposition, when he abruptly got up from his chair and stalked out without a word. I waited for an hour, then went to catch a train to Chicago. I don't think he liked the commercial. The marketing vice president of Sara Lee once twirled in his swivel chair and stared out the window as I sat across from him at his desk. I continued presenting the ads, now having to verbally describe the pictures. Finally I said good-bye to his back and left.

But such behavior is rare. Sure, there's shouting, swearing and fist-banging, but that's normal and desirable when people are intensely involved in a project. Much more dispiriting is the blank stare or noncommittal response to the advertising you've just presented. For the most part, clients are pretty nice people, but no two are alike. Though you can sometimes apply your experience with one client to a specific problem of another, you can never handle two clients in exactly the same way.

Contrary to popular myth, many advertisers have been with their agencies for a long time. Sunkist Growers has been our client since 1906. At least a dozen more have been with the agency longer than I have. In 1973 we celebrated the fiftieth year of our association with the Kimberly-Clark Corporation. However, a new marketing director came in and fired us the following year. Despite such experiences, I am still impressed with the loyalty demonstrated in most client-agency relationships—relationships that, incidentally, involve no real contracts and are usually just informal agreements on the part of each to give the other ninety days' termination notice. Among the most extraordinary examples in FCB's experience is one that involves an equally extraordinary man.

In 1948 Elliston Vinson, FCB's manager on the RKO Pictures account, received a phone call stating that the new owner of RKO wanted to meet him. Thus did Vinson become one of the rare people to actually meet Howard Hughes.

Hughes told Vinson that he intended to get very involved in the advertising for RKO and its releases. He did just that, although in a manner unduplicated by any other client we've ever had. Vinson's phone would ring, and an unidentified voice would say, "Mr. Hughes asks that you keep yourself available. We will call and let you know the exact place and time." Sometime within the next forty-eight hours a second call would specify where and when. The "where" could be the studio, Hughes's bungalow at the Beverly Hills Hotel or a coffee shop. The "when" could be any hour of the night.

Despite these unorthodox aspects of their relationship, Elliston Vinson and Howard Hughes became friends. And advertising became an important factor in the success of many RKO features. At some point early in that friendship, Hughes announced that he not only had interests in a lot of businesses but would probably be getting into many more, and whenever advertising was part of any of them, he wanted Foote, Cone & Belding to be the agency.

Hughes did indeed become involved in many more undertakings, creating what was at one point the largest privately held corporate structure in America. He also became a recluse, the defendant in numerous and enormous lawsuits, and the favorite subject of speculative journalists and fraudulent writers the world over. In 1976, troubled and badgered and ill, Howard Hughes died. Much has changed since those days—or rather, nights—of occult advertising rendezvous between Hughes and Vinson. But the promise has been kept to this day.

Hughes bought TWA and immediately appointed FCB. Only long after he was forced to sell it did we part company with the airline. He gave us the Hughes Tool Company account, which necessitated our opening an office in Houston and losing money year after year. But a deal is a deal, and we served the tool company until the Hughes organization spun it off in December 1972 and we could honorably resign. We still work for Hughes Aircraft Company and Hughes Helicopters, and we worked for Hughes Airwest until it was acquired by Republic Airlines. Assignments came to us automatically, even though Howard Hughes was far off in seclusion at the time and Elliston Vinson had long since retired to Rancho Santa Fe.

No one now active in our company ever laid eyes on Howard Hughes. Fairfax Cone never met him, nor did Lou Scott, who was in charge of our West Coast operations for some fifteen years. I never saw him either, although I felt the effects of his phone calls to managers of his various businesses. When I was creative director in Los Angeles, Surveyor I, which had been designed and built by Hughes Aircraft Company, successfully soft-landed on the moon. It was Thursday evening, June 2, 1966, and though the late TV news was practically dedicated to the event, there was little or no mention of who had created this miraculous machine. Despite the agency's desire to let the world know in advance, the client had decided not to do an advertising campaign pointing out the role of Hughes Aircraft Company. But the next morning we were all summoned to HAC headquarters in Culver City and given forty-eight hours to create and plan a half-million-dollar national advertising effort, including a network television special, to start within a week. Mr. Hughes had been on the phone that night.

Only Elliston Vinson dealt directly with Howard Hughes, and he never talked much about it other than to report decisions. So the contact at the top level was quite meager by normal agency-client standards. Nevertheless, Howard Hughes never forgot his promise. Nor have his successors.

Different clients have different operating styles, and it falls upon the agency to adapt to each. Johnson's Wax and the Clorox Company are highly disciplined, by-the-book marketing organizations where advertising runs a gauntlet of tests. Hallmark is equally successful with a less structured approach.

And each client judges the success of its advertising differently. Some rely heavily on the scores of commercial pre-testing. Sears, being the retailer as well as the manufacturer, is more inclined to watch what happens at the cash register when and where the advertising runs. The Literary Guild pragmatically evaluates every ad on its "cost per order," the cost of running it divided by the number of Guild memberships it produces. Companies such as Borg-Warner can really only gauge the effect of their advertising programs by means of tracking studies that measure awareness levels and attitude changes over time.

Inevitably, however, an advertising program is evaluated in a client's mind by what's happening to his sales during the period in which the advertising runs. Some watch their share of the market, as reported by the A. C. Nielsen Company. Others watch the volume of their shipments from the factory, which, in the case of Lorillard, is measured in millions of units (cigarettes) per day. Bermuda counts the beds occupied in the island's hostelries each night.

Getting new clients is the most frustrating and difficult aspect of our peculiar business, primarily because it really must be done by people who are at the heart of the agency, who can properly represent it and compellingly describe its resources, its talents, its differences and its suitability to the prospect's needs. Obviously, these are the people most occupied with the affairs of present clients. So getting new business is part-time work for extremely busy people.

Then, too, the timing is impossible to predict. We may decide on a dozen or so companies whose business we'd like to have, we may mount massive efforts to persuade them to join our distinguished list of clients, and they may be perfectly content with another agency at the time. But someday—next month? next year? five years from now?—they may suddenly become very discontent. How do we coordinate things? How do we get the timing down right? No single agency has yet come up with the solution. Otherwise there would be only one advertising agency left.

No. On second thought, that couldn't happen because of a peculiar belief maintained by many advertisers that their products shouldn't be handled by an agency that also handles a competitive product. According to this doctrine, one agency cannot accept Company B's toothpaste because it already works on Company A's toothpaste. A stricter interpretation dictates that the agency cannot accept Company B's toothpaste because it works on Company A's mouthwash. And an even stricter interpretation holds that the agency cannot accept Company B's toothpaste because, while it doesn't work on Company A's toothpaste (another agency does), it works on Company A's canned tuna and some oblique treason would be involved. For obvious reasons, this is known in agency circles as "the conflict problem." Curiously enough, companies do not impose such rigorous loyalty tests on their law firms, banks or accounting companies—just their advertising agencies. But it does prevent any one agency from taking over the entire field.

On the whole subject of new business, the best advice I know is contained in the two words Vince Lombardi gave in response to a question about why the Green Bay Packers were so successful: "Defense! Defense!" Other agencies are out after new business, too. And their idea of new business is our old business. So it seems to me the smartest thing to do is to service our present clients and provide them with the most brilliantly thought-out and dazzlingly executed advertising possible. This produces dramatic marketing successes. The client, being only human, brags about them to other manufacturers. Trade publications begin writing about them. The word travels. Our name is mentioned. Suddenly my phone rings. Thus are solved all the problems of conflict, timing, and availability of agency people to go out knocking on doors selling our wares.

Once the phone does ring, a lot of activity commences and a good deal of adrenaline begins flowing. Quite often the next step is to fill out a long questionnaire that asks about the structure and financial condition of the agency, about key personnel and about our creative, media and research philosophies and method of operation. This is the opening move in getting a feel for the agencies an advertiser has selected for screening as he begins narrowing the list down to a workable number.

Next, the advertiser will visit the agencies he's still interested in for what we call a "credentials presentation." Without going too deeply into his business, we try to explain what we're all about and how we would organize to serve him. We show him the work we're doing for present clients and tell him what we think distinguishes us from other agencies. At this session, the advertiser usually spells out what his problems are, why he's looking for a new agency and what he's expecting from it.

If he likes what he sees and hears at this meeting, the advertiser puts us on his "shortlist," usually three to five agencies he has selected to make a final presentation. This presentation can take many forms, involving four or five people from the advertiser side or fifty. I've done them in tiny offices and in big theaters, with elaborate multi-screen audiovisual gadgetry and with simple flip charts. Once I did one with no slides or films; although they were the format of the presentation, the power went out in the prospect's building. Usually this presentation consists of an analysis of the prospect's market, competitive situation and problems, plus an approach to solving those problems. Few sophisticated advertisers these days ask us to present the advertising materials and media plans we would actually recommend. If they do, they allow the time required for such a task, they give us access to all their information and people, and they pay us for our work.

But even when we do present advertising recommendations, other factors play an equal, perhaps more important role. The advertising we proposed to Western Electric ten years ago when we were soliciting their business was superb, if I do say so myself. But I suspect that what really won the account for us was the fact that our people made a tremendous effort to learn about their highly complex business. They visited Western Electric plants, talked to suppliers and customers, did a good deal of consumer research—in short, they immersed themselves in the business. The same was true more recently when we were after the account of Pizza Hut. Among other things, our people went to work in their restaurants, making pizzas and waiting on tables. That's how you come to understand an advertiser's real problems. And this understanding is what he's searching for in an agency.

He's also seeking that ephemeral thing we call "chemistry": an easy, open compatibility with the people who will be assigned to his business. After all, he'll probably be spending more waking hours with them than he does with his wife. He wants to *know* that they're smart, excellent at their jobs, reliable and devoted to his success. But he also wants to *feel* that communication is going to be easy, that they "speak the same language," that the proposed relationship will be exhilarating and, when the tension is high, relieved by humor.

That's why the final presentation should always be constructed around the people who will actually be working on the business, why it must let their personalities shine through all the charts and slides and mechanical trappings that generally characterize such events. The impression that must be left in the prospect's mind is "These people know their business. They've tried hard to know mine. I'd like to work with them." When you do that and do it well, you have yourself a new client.

Some of these considerations also enter into the complex

business of keeping clients once you have them. It's not just a case of doing good advertising. It's not totally dependent on a rising sales curve at the client organization. Agencies have been fired when both these conditions prevailed, Foote, Cone & Belding among them. Such partings are generally blamed on "policy differences" or "dissatisfaction with the creative work," but most of the time they're the result of bad communications. The client asks for something and it never appears. He can't get through to the right level of management at the agency to effect a personnel change on his account. He has the feeling no one is paying attention. Clients can take only so much of this. Or perhaps the agency has slipped into the role of "order taker." It is no longer running out in front of the client with new concepts and daring ideas, urging him forward, but has begun walking beside him merely fulfilling his requests.

Another requisite to keeping clients is total candor. You have to say what you believe. A client who can't accept honest opinions isn't worth having; one who doesn't get them is eventually going to fire his agency. In 1969, when I moved to New York, our operation there was not in the best of health. An appalling amount of business had been lost in the preceding two years, and some of what remained was in trouble. With the invaluable help of a new general manager named Bill Wirth, and with the efforts of many good people, we got back in fighting condition pretty quickly. But during that time I had one particularly memorable experience that demonstrated the value of candor.

One of our large accounts was doing pretty well, but the advertising was not all it should have been. In fact, it got downright embarrassing when the head of the client organization wrote his own campaign for one of the products and made us put it on the air. The man running the account for us had been good in his day but was now drinking too much and doing nothing but taking orders. He was close to retirement, but the client had already indicated, with some urging from our man, that he didn't want to see his buddy leave. All in all, it was a distasteful situation that had me rehearsing a report to the other members of the Executive Committee in which I would tell them how I planned to build the New York operation up again by resigning one of the biggest remaining accounts.

Then a new number-two man came into the client company. By reputation he was a very smart, very tough guy. Would he take over soon? Who would be making the decisions? How should I play it? Before I could make the first move, he called me. I suggested we get together for lunch at the Sky Club on top of the Pan Am Building. I figured if you were going to get fired, you might as well do it in a scenic place.

After a few amenities, he began asking questions. The first was my opinion of the newest campaign. "It's dreadful," I said. "If I had any integrity, I would have resigned the business before I let it run." His expression didn't change. I began thinking about career alternatives. Then he said, "Tell me about your management supervisor on our account." "He was damn good in his day," I said, "but he ought to retire. I'm going to see to it he does in the next two months."

Suddenly my new client let out a laugh that shook the serenity of the Sky Club and turned heads in our direction. "If you'd said anything else," he said, "we were going to have some problems. But, damn it, I think we're going to get along all right." He was running the operation within weeks. There was a new management supervisor on the account. The advertising got much better. So, after a while, did sales. And we get along all right indeed.

EXOTIC VARIETIES

Up to now everything we've talked about, except for some oblique references, has had to do with advertising as part of the marketing of products or services to consumers. And that is what most of the messages you see are all about. But there are many other varieties, some designed for specialized ways of marketing, some designed for very special audiences, and some that involve no product or service at all. In the last category, you'll find political advertising, public service advertising, corporate advertising and an offspring of the latter that in 1974 I named advocacy advertising, perhaps out of a fondness for alliteration.

I was under the impression that these were relatively new genealogical species in the evolution of the craft until I ran across this reference in a booklet published by Lord & Thomas in 1911:

> Another problem in modern advertising is mould-
> ing of public opinion. It may be for the purpose of
> securing a franchise. It may be to win an election. Or
> its purpose may be to renew the good-will of an
> enterprise which has been attacked. One can imag-
> ine, without discussion, what problems like that
> involve.

The problems are still with us. While there are a limited number of competitors to rant and fume when a particular product advertisement appears, anyone with a differing point of view is a competitor when an idea is involved.

I've already unburdened myself of everything I have to say about political advertising in Part I. Let's move quickly on to the

other three varieties. *Public service advertising* is the least controversial of them, but by no means without its detractors. Its
purpose is to enlist public support for a cause deemed to be in
society's best interests by government or by recognized volun-
tary organizations. The time or space, and usually the talent put
into advertising development and execution, are donated by
stations, magazines, newspapers and advertising agencies.

In the United States, the bulk of public service advertising is
coordinated by the Advertising Council, a volunteer association
originally formed during World War II to help the government
win public support for numerous war efforts. Today, among
many other causes, the Council and its volunteer agencies and
media representatives are responsible for campaigns fostering
better understanding of nutrition; warning against environmental pollution, child abuse and energy waste; calling attention to
the dangers of overpopulation, high blood pressure and venereal
disease; and urging the hiring of the handicapped and the support of local United Funds. One of my first copywriting assignments at FCB was the Advertising Council campaign
promoting the purchase of U.S. Savings Bonds. The longest-
lived of all such campaigns is the one for forest fire prevention,
handled by FCB in Los Angeles since 1942.

In 1980, media in the United States contributed time and
space worth close to $600,000,000 to such efforts. Advertising
agencies and advertiser companies donated man-hours and travel
worth additional millions of dollars. What, then, is the controversy about? Since the time and space are free, individuals and
organizations with differing views feel they should receive equal
exposure. The Fairness Doctrine of the Federal Communications Commission encourages them to seek it in broadcast media.
Obviously such demands, if honored, would impose an impossible burden on the media.

A 1975 Advertising Council campaign disseminating information about the American economic system was crippled by an
anti-establishment group, the People's Business Commission,
which wanted equal time to preach what's wrong with the system.
Even our seemingly innocent effort to prevent forest fires has

been challenged by an environmental group which contends that fires, in the long run, benefit a forest.

Corporate advertising may involve a product or service, but it is usually indirect. The purpose is to promote not the company's product but the company itself.

The audiences this advertising seeks to influence are many. Quite often one of them is the company's employees. When their number runs over 100,000 and they're spread across the continent, national advertising is frequently the most efficient as well as the most effective way of providing them with a sense of unity, pride and purpose. Sometimes a company seeks to influence its suppliers with corporate advertising, hoping to convince them that it is a more desirable customer than its competitors. But generally, no matter what the stated purpose, a company goes into corporate advertising to enhance the market value of its stock: to increase awareness and influence attitudes among individual and institutional investors, brokers and security analysts.

All of these are worthy goals and useful purposes for advertising. But they are not easy to achieve, as evidenced by the fact that there are more yawn-producers to be found in this category than in practically any other. In the main, corporate advertising seldom seems to reflect a believable and attractive company personality. It seems unable to demonstrate a sympathetic understanding of the recipient of the message. And it rarely makes any kind of personal, meaningful statement that corresponds with that recipient's needs, wants, problems or self-interest. There are exceptions, but they're rare. Corporate advertising presents great opportunities for agencies capable of seeing the relationships between corporate and consumer realities, relationships so strikingly important that their articulation elicits the response "Hey, they're talking to me."

A fascinating outgrowth of corporate advertising is *advocacy advertising*, which puts forth on behalf of a company a partisan point of view on a controversial subject. It's fascinating because it is pretty much a creature of our times, even though an association of California chain stores used it in 1936 to successfully fight a discriminatory state tax.

JOHN O'TOOLE

The premise is simply this. There are two major forces involved in an increasing number of issues affecting all of us: the
system and the adversary culture. The system is made up of
industries, businesses and financial institutions that provide people with goods, services, jobs and a unique way of life. It's not
perfect. But all in all, it's served us pretty well. The adversary
culture is composed of intellectuals, academics, political activ-
ists, consumer advocates and others who seek basic changes in
the system. They aren't perfect, either. But they aren't always
wrong.

Both groups are fulfilling legitimate and essential functions.
Each seeks to swing public attitudes toward its point of view on
the theory that governmental decisions reflect the will of the
majority. But in these complex and impersonal times, their
campaigns are increasingly waged in the media. So the media
enter the equation as a third element.

It is neither surprising nor entirely reprehensible that the
voice of the adversary culture is more dominant in the media
than that of the system. One role of the press is to question
established institutions, directions and processes. The adversary
culture provides the questions. It deals in crisis and confrontation, the stuff of which news is made. The responses of the
system are seldom characterized by excitement, immediacy or
human interest. Thus the press, by and large, becomes an
advocate for the adversary, leaving advocacy advertising as the
only means of providing a balance.

Advocacy advertising is not, as some critics have charged, an
attempt to control information. Quite the opposite. It adds to
the supply of fact, opinion and interpretation from which the
public shapes its own conclusions. And with issues becoming
increasingly complex, more information has to be better than
less.

Indeed, the issue of advocacy advertising itself has quickly
become more complex. The fear engendered by the Fairness
Doctrine has caused broadcasters and networks to shy away
from commercials that in their view treat controversial subjects.
So stringently have they applied their interpretation of what is

controversial that they've all but ruled out broadcast as a medium for advocacy advertising. But perhaps that's just as well, given the current exigencies of broadcasting. I have doubts as to whether issues as involved as these often are can be fairly or adequately dealt with in a sixty-second commercial, to say nothing of the standard thirty seconds.

In addition, questions have been raised as to whether companies should be allowed to expound their points of view in paid space. The issue may have been resolved by the Supreme Court decision of 1976 extending First Amendment rights to advertising. But then the late Senator Philip A. Hart called for an Internal Revenue Service and Federal Power Commission investigation of oil companies and utilities, claiming that their advocacy advertising was not a legitimate business expense and should be paid for with after-tax dollars. The American Association of Advertising Agencies filed a position paper with the Hart subcommittee, pointing out that this kind of advertising is a requisite of corporate social responsibility. The question is still unresolved.

So the path is not without its brambles. Still, a growing number of companies and associations have been engaging in advocacy advertising in the last few years. An interesting example was a 1974 ad signed by the employees of Pan American Airways seeking public support for their beleaguered employer. It spoke of the governmental policies that place Pan Am at a competitive disadvantage against foreign carriers, including the fact that a foreign nation can purchase a U.S.-made jet for substantially less than Pan Am can. Some of these things we had heard before, but they became more credible, more personally involving, when presented by a group of hardworking people concerned about their jobs.

The American Electric Power Company launched a campaign early on in the fuel crisis advocating the exploitation of our coal resources as a partial answer. The series was characterized by rational, well-documented, persuasive arguments and by that rarest of all virtues in this field, consistency. But to my way of thinking, it was marred by the manner in which it sought to involve the casual reader. It chose to set up a "villain," the oil-rich, insidious Arab sheik.

By and large, advocacy advertising has belonged to the oil companies, and the quality has varied considerably. The best examples have communicated, through subject matter, copy style and graphics, a unique, credible, personal identity for the company. People listen to, and buy from, someone they know and trust and can recognize. This holds as true for an idea as for a product. The good advocacy ads have also been based on a healthy respect for the reader's intelligence. Flag-waving, posturing and preaching the virtues of the free enterprise system are not going to work today; facts and persuasive reasoning will. And these ads have sought to interest, involve and persuade the reader in terms of his own life and the things that are important to him. Simply shouting "foul" won't do that. Throwing a bunch of numbers at him in a headline won't do it. Talking solely about earnings and costs won't do it. But talking to him about *his* costs might. Talking to him about *his* needs and *his* home and *his* family might. And since most public issues are directly related to those things, you can involve him personally in the company's problems and programs because in a sense they are his as well.

In September 1980, Opinion Research Corporation published the results of the first opinion poll I had seen on advocacy advertising. The degree of public acceptance was surprising. Of the 1,010 people interviewed, 90% claimed to have heard or read such a message. Of those, 68% found this kind of advertising believable, 64% said it helped them understand a particular issue, and 57% allowed as how it even led them to change their minds about it. Even more surprising was the finding that 85% of the respondents felt that corporations should be allowed to use television to disseminate their opinions on controversial public issues.

It's difficult to draw many general conclusions about the three forms of nonproduct advertising we've been discussing, but I'll venture two. First, all are more effectively handled in the print media. Issues and ideas still seem to be the province of rational persuasion, which requires the development and specificity afforded only by the printed word. The customary lengths of television spots encourage oversimplification and a retreat into impressionism. Even public service broadcast messages are used primarily as "reminder" advertising, or they request that the listener or viewer write in for a printed booklet. Second, success in any of the three depends upon meticulous attention to every stage of the developmental process: strategy, idea and execution. Most failures can be attributed to a headlong emotional plunge into the last stage.

As I've noted, the distinguishing feature of public service, corporate and advocacy advertising is that they involve no particular product or service. But the skills and knowledge they require are readily available in general consumer-product advertising agencies, and that's where such accounts are primarily served today. Other varieties of advertising—those that stem from specialized techniques of marketing or that focus on a specialized audience—are usually the province of specialized agencies. In the former category (or in either, for that matter) the largest by far is *direct response advertising*.

Direct response is clearly part of a specialized kind of marketing since it eliminates all the distribution systems between the advertiser and the customer, replacing them with the U.S. Postal Service. The advertisement is the only salesman. If the prospect is turned into a customer by the ad, he cuts out the coupon, fills it in, writes out a check and sends the two to the company. His purchase is mailed to him directly. There are variations of all kinds on this model. More and more, credit card numbers are being accepted in lieu of checks. Many direct marketers use television commercials, often requesting the prospect to place a toll-free call to an agent who takes the credit card number, name and address.

There are two kinds of direct response marketing: media/direct response, which we've just been discussing, and direct mail/direct response, which involves no ads or commercials at all. The latter works by sending brochures to everyone on a particular mailing list. Once that brochure is in the prospect's hands, the process is the same as though he had been reached by an ad.

Media direct response is of interest to those outside the specialty because it's the only kind of media advertising that can be evaluated by a single, reliable number: the cost of running the ad divided by the responses received. Furthermore, "split runs" can be employed to test the pulling power of one headline or illustration over another. Direct response is the only kind of advertising that is directly related to sales and allows no excuses for poor results. Professional critics who decry advertising as an economic waste have difficulty jousting with the results of media direct response.

It is estimated that in 1978 $7 billion was spent in the United States on direct response advertising, divided about equally between media and direct mail. Some of the biggest hitters in the business are American Express, the Literary Guild, Book-of-the-Month, Merrill Lynch, CBS Publications, Columbia House and Encyclopedia Britannica. Though the field is dominated by specialized agencies, many of those have been acquired by and are operating as subsidiaries of the big general agencies.

Directory or Yellow Pages advertising is another subspecies designed, like direct response, to fit a specialized kind of marketing. Many companies, especially those who sell through agents, dealers and franchises, conclude their advertising messages with "Check in the Yellow Pages for the dealer nearest you." When you do, or when you just happen to need a widget and let your fingers do the walking through the "W's," those companies want to catch your eye. Directory advertising agencies design display listings for them in order to relate the advertised product or service to the addresses and phone numbers of the people who sell it. The agency also buys space in as many of the directories as needed, pays for the space at the lowest possible rate and performs diverse other services.

There's more than a billion dollars' worth of Yellow Pages advertising done in the United States each year. The five biggest clients are U-Haul, Chevrolet, General Electric, Hertz and Ryder Trucks. Moving companies, airlines, finance companies and insurance companies are also big spenders in this category. Of the five largest Yellow Pages advertising agencies, two are owned by general agencies: Wahlstrom & Co. of Stamford, Connecticut, is part of Foote, Cone & Belding, and Ketchum Yellow Pages of Pittsburgh belongs to KM&G, International.

The remaining special varieties address certain specific audiences. Two of them speak to consumer markets, but their role is rather small at the moment. One is *entertainment advertising*. In recent years agencies have been formed to serve the unique needs of theatrical and motion picture producers as they become more and more sophisticated in marketing their "products." The other is *ethnic advertising*. A number of shops sprang up in the early seventies claiming a special understanding of the black community and a unique expertise in persuading blacks and reaching them with media. Few have prospered. The Spanish-language agencies that appeared about the same time have fared better. Translating national campaigns or preparing special ones for the growing Hispanic markets in New York, Chicago, Florida and the Southwest, these agencies show signs of becoming an important part of the action. As evidence, the larger general agencies have begun buying them or luring their principals away to start subsidiaries.

Three other special varieties are not in touch with the consumer at all. One is what has come to be called *business-to-business advertising*, a catchall term for what we used to call industrial and trade advertising. Business-to-business advertising is a message from one manufacturer to another who might need the product or service to produce another product or service. Or it is a message from a manufacturer to the dealer or retailer who sells his product to the consumer. Such messages may appear as ads in business or trade publications or in the form of direct mail. The business press in America took in almost $2 billion in advertising revenue in 1980.

A great deal of business-to-business advertising is done right in the general agencies. J. Walter Thompson and BBDO are among the leaders in this category, although it accounts for less than 5% of the total volume of each. A number of agencies specialize in it, but none exclusively. To further complicate the issue, some of the specialist agencies have been acquired by general agencies; for example, Marsteller by Young & Rubicam, and Aitkin-Kynett by Foote, Cone & Belding.

Recruitment advertising, on the other hand, is highly specialized. Few general agencies try it; fewer succeed at it. This doesn't mean we aren't interested, however. Foote, Cone & Belding acquired the highly respected firm of Deutsch, Shea & Evans in 1980; J. Walter Thompson owns the World Wide Agency; Doyle Dane Bernbach purchased half interest in Bernard Hodes Advertising.

Recruitment advertising is a message from a company that needs certain skills or talents to an individual who has them. It used to be called "Help Wanted" advertising until its market extended to big-ticket executives and engineers and the ads became much larger and more sophisticated. It involves a difficult kind of persuasion. As Arnold Deutsch tells me, all you're trying to do is persuade a happy, successful guy to quit his job and move his wife, who loves her present house, and his kids, who've just made the high school football team and cheerleading squad, to a strange city where some boss who doesn't like him might can him in six months. But it's a growing category, up 25.7% in 1979 over 1978. Spending is running over $2 billion, 90% to 95% of it in newspapers. Some of the major recruitment advertisers are American Airlines, AT&T, Boeing, Exxon and IBM.

As recruitment advertising is a kind of business-to-business advertising, so too is *financial advertising*. At least I define it that way, yielding to the reality that most banks use general consumer agencies to advertise the financial services they offer to the public. So, increasingly, do the large stockbrokers like Merrill Lynch, E. F. Hutton and Smith Barney. The commercial assignments of the banks, however, and the institutional business of the stockbrokerages are often turned over to financial advertising agencies.

The two major agencies in this specialty are Doremus & Co., now a subsidiary of BBDO, and Albert Frank/FCB. Both are situated right in the Wall Street area. Both have widened their sights to include financially oriented direct response and public relations as the larger general agencies have taken over the consumer business of their major clients. But both remain the experts in financial notice, or, as it's more commonly and graphically called, "tombstone" advertising.

Tombstone ads are those intimidating masses of type, enclosed by borders, that you frequently see in the financial section of the newspaper announcing a public offering of stocks or bonds. One investment banking house is usually the leader, with as many as a dozen others participating. The order in which these names appear is of great importance to the firms. The nature and wording of the information is of great importance to the Securities and Exchange Commission. No mistakes or typographical errors are countenanced. Deadlines are short, often overnight, and the ads must appear in all the publications the schedule calls for—simultaneously. It's a tricky business and demands technical expertise. It's also a profitable business for the agencies.

Finally there's *pharmaceutical or health care advertising*. This is a kind of business-to-business advertising, too, since the audience is made up primarily of physicians and hospital administrators. The media are medical journals and direct mail. The advertisers are the major drug manufacturers, such as American Home Products, Ciba-Geigy, Hoffman–La Roche, Pfizer and Merck. The subject matter is information and news about their products, particularly new drugs, both those sold over the counter and those available only by prescription. The objective, obviously, is to persuade hospitals to order them and physicians to prescribe them.

Health care advertising is highly technical as well as fraught with legal problems. It requires an unusual breed of copywriter, someone with substantial scientific or medical training. Since this kind of background does not frequently arrive in the same package with writing skills and primary process thinking, recruitment is a constant problem in health care advertising agencies. Though it's impossible to put an accurate dollar figure on the size of this specialty, I suspect total expenditures for media and direct mail are close to a billion dollars. Of the ten leading agencies in the field, four are subsidiaries of general agencies. That includes the biggest, Sudler & Hennessey, which is owned by Young & Rubicam.

This brief tour through the botanical gardens of advertising, identifying and labeling exotic species, demonstrates that there's more to the craft than just mouthwash commercials. And perhaps there's something else to be learned. No form of advertising is entirely free from criticism—either by the professional critics or by those to whom it's directed—but there is one group of specialized varieties that seems to incur very little. I have never heard anyone say that a business-to-business ad or a recruitment ad or a commercial banking ad or a medical journal ad was annoying. Or that it was boring. Or that it insulted his intelligence.

Granted, television is not the medium for these messages, so some of the potential pitfalls are absent from the start. But I think it goes beyond media. These are the varieties that don't speak to a consumer audience. The market, in each case, is smaller and more defined. It is professional, well educated and quite knowledgeable about the subject. The writer probably feels he knows the individuals he's talking to pretty well, and indeed, he does know quite a few of them personally. He's not going to be irrelevant, corny, boring or offensive with someone whose opinion he respects, someone to whom the subject is so familiar and important.

If every advertising person—on both the agency side and the client side—felt the same way about the consumer he's addressing, there wouldn't be enough violations of the implicit contract to put in Ralph Nader's eye.

ADVERTISING ABROAD

The advertising agency and modern approaches to advertising were invented in the United States, but they quickly moved out across the world. In fact, they became one of our most successful exports. No other country matches the United States either in dollar volume or in percentage of national income spent on advertising, but some are getting closer in the latter category. We spend 2% of our gross national product on advertising (a percentage that, as we've noted, has not changed since 1925), Switzerland spends 1.33%, Canada 1.21%, England 1.19%, Brazil 1.13%, Japan .88% and West Germany .83%.

Like other American innovations, advertising has found skilled technicians abroad who have become as adept as the originators and have adapted the basic principles to local situations. As yet, however, no overseas adapter has turned the tables and successfully marketed its version in the United States, as has happened with that most notable of American brainchildren, the automobile. Indeed, in almost every important world market, the leading agency is U.S.-based or U.S.-affiliated. Of the top ten in West Germany, only one is not. In the United Kingdom, just three in that prestigious circle are not.

But this does not mean the American practitioner can simply get off the plane and start doing things as he did them back on Park or Michigan Avenue. The differences are many, the hazards formidable and the mistakes costly. For example, though it's always important to know your prospect, in a foreign context it's even more so; ignorance of the people you're talking to, of their beliefs and customs, can be very embarrassing. Transplanted American creative people always want to photograph European men kissing women's hands. But they seldom know that the nose must never touch the hand, or that this rite is reserved solely for married women. And how do you know the woman in the photograph is married? By the ring on her left hand, of course. Well, in Spain, Denmark, Holland and Germany, Catholic women wear the wedding ring on the right hand.

When photographing a couple entering a restaurant or theater, you show the woman preceding the man, correct? No. Not in Germany and France. And this would be laughable in Japan. Having someone in a commercial hold up his hand with the back of it to you, the viewer, and the fingers moving toward him should communicate "come here." In Italy it means "goodbye." And that seasonal advertising standby Santa Claus is not exactly the same elsewhere. Although he came to the United States from Germany, he doesn't bring gifts there. It's the Christ child who does Germans that kindness. It's Father Christmas in England, and an ugly old lady named La Befana in Italy. Furthermore, in most other countries the gifts arrive on Epiphany, January 6, rather than on Christmas Day.

A woman in Sweden is not interested in hiding gray hair from her husband, but she is eager to conceal it from her employer. This is important if you're advertising hair color in Scandinavia, just as it's important to know that 15% of the women in Denmark smoke cigars, should you be advertising tobacco products there. And if you're advertising coffee, it's essential to know that instant coffee is eschewed in Sweden as a sign of a lazy housewife. In England, on the other hand, instant coffee is about the only kind you can get. But when an advertiser tried to sell the English an instant tea, he lost his shirt. One doesn't toy with the British tea ritual.

Many unsuccessful product introductions overseas probably wouldn't have occurred if the American marketers had learned more about the local consumer. Jell-O failed in Denmark because it's too light to be taken seriously as a dessert. A cake mix bombed out in Belgium because it based its advertising on the superiority of homemade over store-bought cake. This was ridiculous to Belgians, whose standard of excellence and elegance was the cake from the local baker. Deodorant soaps have never succeeded in Europe, where body odors are considered rather sexy. A brand of frozen fish selling at half the price of fresh fish never got off the ground in Spain. There weren't enough refrigerators. A brand of cigarettes named Windsor didn't make it in Denmark because that was the name of the leading toilet paper.

Understanding such cultural differences is essential to advertising effectively abroad. It is also a fascinating and rewarding pursuit. Few things in advertising have given me more joy than the friendships and new vistas I've found by working in an international company and learning about the countries in which we do business. I've learned French, Italian and German to speed the process. Also because I don't think anyone has any business criticizing advertising unless he understands it. Also because I always wanted to read Verlaine, Dante and Schiller in the original.

But I still don't know enough about any of those cultures or any of those national populations to personally create advertising for them. That's why each overseas FCB operation is staffed and run by people from that country, people who are attuned to the moods and sensitivities and forces of tradition that affect the responses of the population to communication stimuli, who constantly study their country and their countrymen in search of the most accurate understanding of them, just as we do in the United States. What I can do, however, is work with the people in our overseas operations, combining their knowledge of the market and their considerable talents with whatever I've learned about the basics of this craft over the years. And in doing so, I've observed some interesting differences in the business of advertising in those countries as contrasted with ours.

The advertising agency itself is pretty much the same the world over, having been modeled on the structure developed here. The most dramatic difference is in Japan, where they do not recognize what I referred to earlier as "the conflict problem." Japanese agencies tend to specialize in the various media, buying up big blocks of time or space and enjoying a virtual monopoly on the best that's available. Thus, one agency can, and does, handle

four competitive automobile accounts, but often only the television or radio or newspaper portions. Because it is free of the
growth restrictions imposed by the conflict problem in other
countries, the biggest agency in Japan, Dentsu, is also the
biggest agency in the world, with billings and income substantially larger than those of Young & Rubicam or J. Walter
Thompson. But it's just a matter of time until Dentsu, with 97%
of its business in one country, yields first place to a truly
international agency with business emanating from twenty or
more countries.

Among Western nations, the major differences in advertising
have to do with the role of television. Where there is no television advertising, as is the case in the Scandinavian countries, the
business is smaller and the advertising process takes longer to
achieve results. In France and Italy, where commercial time is
limited and announcements are run in blocks several times a
day, television is a factor in advertising, but far less so than in
the United States.

Socialist governments and strong socialist parties also make a
difference. In general, efforts to control the content of advertising increase in direct proportion to the power of the socialist
party. In Sweden the government has forced an end to the
commission system of agency compensation, and agencies now
bid against one another for advertising "jobs." The government
also taxes certain kinds of advertising and controls what can and
can't be said or done in advertising for many product categories,
most notably for cigarettes. France enacted a number of restrictions on cigarette advertising in 1976. In Italy we had to change
a commercial in which a housewife was given 50,000 lire for a
towel to be used in a detergent demonstration because the
exchange was deemed "capitalistic" by government controllers.

Needless to say, American advertising people feel most at
home in English-speaking advertising environments. They have
more staying power, too. There's nothing as disorienting as not
understanding what people around you are saying; there's nothing as tedious as trying to do business through a translator; and
even if you're fairly proficient in the language, there's nothing as

212

brain-wearying as the first few days of actually working in it.

But even other English-speaking countries present subtle differences in approach to the craft. In the past, Canadian advertising was as close to the American variety as you could get; historically, many ads and commercials for products marketed in both countries were simply shipped north and run in Canadian publications and on Canadian stations with minor adaptations. But that changed considerably during the seventies, when nationalism burgeoned in Canada.

Canadian companies that advertise in Canadian editions of *Time*, *Reader's Digest* and other U.S. publications using essentially the same editorial matter as their American counterparts cannot claim the cost as a business expense for tax purposes. The government has introduced regulations banning U.S.-produced photographs and films for Canadian use. In fact, when I'm carrying U.S. commercials to discuss with FCB people in Canada, I have a harder time getting through customs in Toronto than I do crossing into East Berlin. All this has affected advertising approaches. It is no longer an advantage to indicate that the product is manufactured in America or is the most popular in America, or even to allude to its American heritage.

Another factor in Canadian advertising is the country's bilingualism. Not only must products be labeled in French and English, but television commercials have to be produced in both languages. This adds to the cost of production and also limits the approaches that can be considered. Sometimes separate strategies are required for Quebec and the rest of Canada.

Thus, although it's an ocean away and is a much smaller country whose English, being the King's, often differs markedly from ours in accent and syntax, England produces the closest thing to the U.S. variety of advertising. When it's silly and self-conscious, it's as embarrassing as the worst you see here. But more often—in fact, more frequently than in the United States—it's well thought out, has an imaginative and relevant idea, and is simply and professionally executed. Right now, England is turning out the best advertising in the world.

A few of the classics I keep in my drawer are from the United

Kingdom. One is a birth control poster that makes its point to men by featuring an enormously pregnant male. Another is an ad directed to young women in an effort to recruit candidates for nurses' training. The illustration shows several young doctors and nurses in an earnest and apparently crucial consultation. The headline reads: "When's the last time anyone at the office asked your opinion?"

Australians travel and work abroad more than any people I know. Many advertising types down there have worked in London agencies, so there is a British quality to Australian advertising. But in recent years a unique character has become apparent: a saltiness, a lack of pretension, an irreverence that seems to me—a dedicated fan of Australia since my first visit in 1968—quite in keeping with the national personality. Much of it has to do with casting. Actors and presenters no longer sound like they came directly from Oxford. They are unmistakably Australian, and the way they phrase the copy points takes full advantage of the hearty and earthy Australian humor.

This new character might have been born in 1972 with a series of commercials for Winfield cigarettes. The first one I saw featured a gentleman in elegant formal attire, in an equally elegant setting, preparing to tell us about the product. When he began speaking, it was with the words, inflection and harsh accent of the Australian working bloke. The presenter was a bridge painter named Paul Hogan, who became famous overnight, as did the slogan he grated out: "Any'ow, 'ave a Winfield." Australian advertising hasn't been quite the same since. Happily.

South African advertising has not yet reached the state of the art—if you'll forgive the phrase—achieved in other English-speaking countries, but it's moving fast. And then, South Africa is not, strictly speaking, an English-speaking country. There is another official language, Afrikaans. In addition, there are seven Bantu dialects, each incomprehensible to those who speak another. The language problems make those faced in Canada seem simple. In print advertising, they necessitate several versions of an ad, depending on whether the publication is printed in

English, Afrikaans or Bantu. This is costly but achievable.

Television came to South Africa early in 1976. At present English and Afrikaans programming appear on alternate nights. I think it's important that the Bantu dialects somehow be accommodated, that the enormous black population be brought into the consumer market, thereby creating the kind of mass production of quality goods at low prices that has raised the standard of living in every other country where it's been realized. When that happens, South Africa could be one of the world's great advertising centers. More important, some of its serious social problems might be on the way to solution.

France is a nation that, for reasons beyond my meager comprehension of socio-history, has always seemed torn between an innate sense of order and an equally innate attraction to chaos. This observation is not meant to be critical, for I am one of those who still love strolling the streets of Paris at any hour of any season. But the implicit dichotomy of Descartes, DeGaulle and Napoleon on the one hand, and Robespierre, Rimbaud and the riots of 1968 on the other, is inescapable. And this dichotomy is apparent in French advertising.

I subscribe to five French magazines and read a good many more. I would have to describe much of the advertising I see as chaotic, as I would the television commercials I watch when I'm there. Too much of it is, strangely enough, borrowed from American formats that have become hackneyed and strident even in their native land. In marked contrast is the work of an agency formerly called Impact—a fitting name, since that is what it has had on the French advertising scene. So interesting did I and my associates find this work that we sought out its owner and founder, Pierre Lemonnier, and today the agency is Impact-FCB.

Lemonnier's magazine advertisements follow no set pattern, but they stand out from others by virtue of their simple elegance, their adherence to rules of layout and typography, and the meticulous perfection of the photography. Each is an executional gem. But a more important difference stems from the point of view about the consumer that underlies the thinking and planning of Impact-FCB work. Lemonnier believes that aggressive, loud advertising repels the prospect. He seeks to create messages that attract rather than pursue. He feels that an advertisement is far more effective when the reader comes to it, rather than it chasing the reader. Thus, an Impact-FCB ad is, in most French magazines today, an oasis of reason and taste where the product is clearly presented and its benefits to the prospect fully explained. Others are beginning to emulate what is now called the Impact "style," and this, in my view, is what characterizes French advertising today: a sea of brash, U.S.-spawned approaches, dotted with islands of inviting rationality and simplicity. Chaos and order.

The Impact style is now becoming apparent in our work in Italy, where Pierre's own influence and that of a copy-writer he trained, added to the formidable talents of our Milan creative director, Michel Burton, and our creative director for all of Italy, Umberto Savoia, has brought to our advertising a quality and symmetry that make it unusual in its environment.

Italy and its people are close to my heart. It seems to me they deserve far better than they receive from their government and most of their advertising agencies. There is a tawdriness to much Italian advertising, a lack of elegance, that doesn't fit with the art and literature, the architecture, the sense of design that characterizes everything else in Italian life. One of the most popular advertising formats is a sort of photographic comic strip with balloons emanating from the mouths of gullible house-wives; it is generally a thing of monumental ugliness.

For many years, a fascinating aberration of Italian television advertising was *Carosello*, a fifteen-minute nightly segment com-posed totally of commercial messages, two minutes and fifteen seconds each. The rules dictated that the product could not be seen, mentioned or alluded to in the first one minute and forty seconds of the film. Then it had to flow naturally from the sheer entertainment that preceded it. Some of the best creative minds in the country were at work on the *caroselli*, and the result was the most popular program on Italian TV. Needless to say, as Communist party influence in government increased, *Carosello*

216

was taken off the air. As for the standard Italian commercials, however, it is difficult to reconcile the bulk of the film work with the culture that produced Fellini and Antonioni.

Italy is the only country in which FCB people have gone out on strike. They did so with great reluctance when ordered to by the union, which had some vague grievance with several other large international agencies. Being considered members of management, the directors of the company could enter the office. Since they represented all the skills and disciplines of the agency, they managed somehow to keep the major work flowing. Throughout they received much encouragement, plus *caffé* and *panini*, from their striking brethren outside.

The advertising agency business in Germany may be more like the business in the United States than is that of any other country. It's booming; it's producing new product successes; it uses television in much the same way we do; it's diversifying from pure media advertising into public relations, sales promotion, recruitment advertising, pharmaceutical advertising and many other specialized areas. And the salaries of top professionals in Germany are comparable to those paid in large New York and Chicago agencies.

Yet the advertising itself is strangely different. Announcers shout more than they do in other northern European countries. There is a greater reliance on gratuitous nudity—the "nipple and navel" school of illustration—than in the Latin countries. Layout and typography were once pretty heavy-handed but have begun to improve—particularly, I'm happy to add, in the work of FCB. But the difference is more in the spirit, the general approach of German advertising, than in its physical execution. There is a coolness, a remoteness, a "you and me" as opposed to a "we" attitude about it. When humor enters in, it is more a gag than a shared smile. There is, if I may say so, little love in it.

I've discussed this perception with my creative comrades in Frankfurt, and most agree. Some say it's the state of development, that U.S. advertising once gave the same impression and that eventually, as product categories grow more competitive,

German advertising will gravitate towards "maker's marks" based on warm, appealing identities. Others tell me it is a reflection of the German character, that overt displays of emotion or affection would be laughed at. I don't know which explanation is accurate, but since no one else does either, I'm going to accept the former.

You might expect to encounter a similar phenomenon up in the cold Scandinavian climes. Not so. Swedish advertising, while exhibiting a certain classic but pleasing severity in typography, is rife with warm, human faces, with headlines that strike a personal chord and with situations that compel you to enter by virtue of their honesty and reality. And though there is no commercial television in Sweden, many of the films I've seen for cinema advertising are superlative productions, direct and involving and worthy of claiming common parentage with Ingmar Bergman.

Nor is there much to be found in Danish advertising that is cool or remote. Here the graphic style is, perhaps, freer and more experimental than in Sweden, but the same humanity and empathy surface in much of the work. In addition, the natural humor of the Danes encourages some of the most intricate wordplays I've ever seen cavorting about in headlines.

Humor in Dutch advertising, on the other hand, has gone so far in recent years as to render the message, even the product, a total mystery in many cases. The egocentric excesses that dominated the American advertising scene in the sixties have, like some virus that leaps an ocean after debilitating a national population, invaded Holland. Pratfalls and pies-in-the-face abound. And, as was the case in the United States during the plague, advertising awards have become overwhelmingly important to agency people. These awards are generally bestowed upon commercials and ads that draw the biggest laugh from an audience of advertising people. It goes without saying that FCB creative people in Holland are of a different persuasion. The advertising they turn out is by any standards some of the best being done anywhere in the world today.

I have been concentrating here on differences. Perhaps too

much. While they certainly exist, while I would be surprised if the same executional approach was equally effective with the playful population of Hong Kong—obsessed with gambling and auguries of health and luck—and the diligent, systematic citizenry of Hamburg, the differences are encountered most frequently and dramatically on the social surface. As you dig deeper, they diminish and eventually disappear the closer you approach the essence of the individual human being.

There is, for me, one overriding experience in this regard. I have shown a particular commercial—the Hallmark spot in which a secretary goes through a rotten day that is finally brightened when she gets home and finds that someone has remembered her with a card—in fourteen countries to people speaking eight different languages. In each case, the audience has broken out in spontaneous applause.

Armed with talent, a grasp of the fundamentals and a dedication to truly understanding and entering the lives of the people, one could effectively practice the craft of advertising in any country we've mentioned. Unfortunately it's the latter that too many American advertising *emigrés* fail at. They live in American ghettos, replicate American meals and communicate in the American language. They drive to and from work rather than enter the rich and revealing worlds of the London, Paris, Milan, Tokyo or Frankfurt subways at rush hour. They seek relief at the American Club rather than seeking understanding in the homes of the people who are the society.

At one time, the most striking difference between advertising in the United States and advertising in other countries, particularly the European ones, was the degree of governmental regulation. Recent activities of our Federal Trade Commission and other regulatory bodies have diminished the differences, but there is still greater freedom here in terms of what we can say as well as what we can say it about.

A number of governments have attempted to discourage the use of certain products by banning advertising for them. This seems to me not only unfair but intrinsically inefficient and even dishonest. If the government deems the product injurious to the

219

JOHN O'TOOLE

well-being of the population, it should ban the sale, not the advertising, of that product. To ban the advertising is merely a cosmetic action that satisfies certain activist groups without sacrificing the tax revenues and jobs involved. Furthermore, experience after experience demonstrates that it doesn't work. Cigarette advertising has been banned in Italy since 1962. Cigarette consumption has actually increased since that date. Advertising for alcoholic beverages has not been allowed in Sweden since July 1979, yet that country still experiences one of the highest incidences of alcoholism outside the Soviet Union, where, obviously, there is no advertising for liquor either. Advertising is simply salesmanship. When it is legal to sell a product, it should be legal to advertise it.

Equally disturbing and ineffective is government regulation of how an advertisement can and cannot be made, regulation having nothing to do with matters of truth and accuracy. In a number of countries, people cannot be depicted in cigarette advertisements. Government functionaries who believe witchcraft is a major element in advertising perceive some logic in this, but those of us who understand how advertising works know it accomplishes little. In West Germany and France it is forbidden to compare any aspect of your product's performance with that of any competitor, even an unnamed one. In the United States, the FTC encourages comparison and the naming of the compared brand. Both governments claim to be acting in the best interests of the consumer.

Attempts on the part of governments to regulate the content of advertising show no signs of abating, particularly in Europe. They are responses to groups of professional critics who, like their counterparts in the United States, are less opposed to advertising than to the fundamental concepts of a free marketplace and freedom of choice. Those who value these freedoms, along with freedom of expression, can only prevail by separating the professional critics from their popular support, by demonstrating to the consumer that advertising contributes to his well-being and is responsive to his expressed expectations. The implicit contract knows no national boundaries.

220

RESPONSIBILITIES

Every business has responsibilities to a number of publics, all of which weigh heavily. But the advertising business has a uniquely complex set.

Most advertising agencies are corporations and have responsibilities to their shareholders. Much has been written about the difference between agencies whose shares are held privately and those whose stock is available to the public. FCB's shares are traded on the New York Stock Exchange; it was first of the large agencies to go public. Now seven more of the top twelve agencies I identified earlier have followed suit.

Personally, I see little difference in the management of public and privately held agencies and no difference in their responsibilities. No matter who the owners, the agency has an obligation to maintain an operation they can be proud of, to make a profit on their investment, to reinvest a reasonable amount in the business and to keep its most important asset—its people—well rewarded and motivated. Since more than half of FCB's shares are owned by employees or ex-employees, we're not likely to forget that obligation.

Another responsibility is to the client who's paying the bills—most obviously, to spend his money wisely. That means, of course, getting the best value out of every dollar spent on media. It also means squeezing maximum quality out of every supplier of research, film production, photography, type, engravings, music and art. Though it's hard work, this part of the job makes you very popular. What doesn't is persuading a client to maintain his level of advertising while he's being besieged from above with demands to cut expenditures. What doesn't is

221

persuading him to stick with a campaign that's working when everyone around him is saying it's time for something new. These pleas can appear self-serving, but they can often save a client far more in the long run than any economies you could effect in his production budget.

Everyone involved in developing advertising is responsible to the client for applying the creative multiplier to the strategy statement; for maintaining his maker's mark from ad to ad, campaign to campaign and medium to medium; and for seeking out and eliminating errors that would make him look foolish or statements that could get him in trouble. But the most important responsibility to the client is to represent the consumer's point of view. The client is immersed in the manufacturing, the selling to the trade and the shipping of the product; he has difficulty stepping away and seeing it objectively. We have to stay inside the consumer's head.

There is yet another responsibility, less often considered but no less important, to the media in which the messages appear. As noted earlier, no one buys a magazine or newspaper, no one turns on the radio or television, principally for the advertising. Advertising reaches the prospect only as a result of the goodwill the medium has attained with him. We have to recognize the limitations of that goodwill and do nothing to endanger it.

Long ago, in a more genteel era, the *New Yorker* turned down a campaign for Dial soap because the words "perspiration odor" appeared in the copy. I've never seen Fax Cone get as steamed up or argue so vehemently. But the *New Yorker* held to its position—though it meant giving up substantial advertising dollars—and Fax ended up unhappy but with a lifelong admiration for the publishers.

The readers are the magazine's; the viewers or listeners are the station's. They subscribe or tune in because they like what they get. Advertising has a responsibility to encourage editorial excellence and, in the process, to arrive at some understanding of the people each medium reaches and what aspects of their lives each touches to produce the relationship on which advertis-

ing messages travel. Any pressure we put on editors or broadcasters to change their product against their will is self-destructive.
Any attempt to influence a medium's editorial policy with the
weight of a client's advertising dollars should get the perpetrator
fired on the spot.

The First Amendment to the Constitution, guaranteeing freedom of the press, is a valuable possession and in today's world a
disturbingly rare one. And it is an advertising practitioner's bread
and butter. Its guarantees have, up until quite recently, been
ours only through their application to the media. In its decision
of May 24, 1976, the Supreme Court extended First Amendment protections to advertising. But it's important to examine
the tone and wording of the decision, as delivered by Justice
Blackmun. For example:

> Advertising, however tasteless and excessive it some-
> times may seem, is nonetheless dissemination of in-
> formation as to who is producing and selling what
> product, for what reason, and at what price. So long
> as we preserve a predominantly free enterprise econ-
> omy, the allocation of our resources in large measure
> will be made through numerous private economic
> decisions.
>
> It is a matter of public interest that those deci-
> sions, in the aggregate, be intelligent and well
> informed.
>
> To this end, the free flow of commercial informa-
> tion is indispensable. And if it is indispensable to the
> proper allocation of resources in a free enterprise
> system, it is also indispensable to the formation of
> intelligent opinions as to how that system ought to be
> regulated or altered. Therefore, even if the First
> Amendment were thought to be primarily an instru-
> ment to enlighten public decision-making in democ-
> racy, we could not say that the free flow of informa-
> tion does not serve that goal.

Clearly the extension of First Amendment privileges to advertising is somewhat reluctantly, if not conditionally, bestowed. If more evidence is needed, here is Calvin Collier, chairman of the Federal Trade Commission, commenting on the Court's decision:

> Untruthful speech, commercial or otherwise, has never been protected for its own sake. Obviously, much commercial speech is not provably false, or even wholly false, but only deceptive or misleading. We foresee no obstacle to a state's dealing with this problem. The First Amendment, as we construe it today, does not prohibit the state from insuring that the stream of commercial information flows cleanly as well as freely.

Our primary resonsibility to the media is to be sure that nothing we do—or fail to do—abuses those privileges the Supreme Court has extended to us and the Constitution has guaranteed to them.

All these responsibilities touch inevitably on another, the most important in terms of advertising's survival—our responsibility to the consumer. Obviously we are obliged to provide him or her with truthful information about the advertised product or service. But this obligation goes beyond those shaky semantical platforms, those toeholds in the edge of verity that lawyers will pass as "defendable." Fairfax Cone warned about this sort of thing more than a decade ago when he wrote,

> The blatant lie is banned. But there is a kind of scrupulous dishonesty abroad in advertising, and particularly in television advertising, that could pull the whole house down.
>
> One of these days someone is going to explain and expose the weasel. The weasel is the flaw in the promise that makes it no promise at all, and thus legal.
>
> No matter what the commercials say, it is impossible for all synthetic detergents to cut dishpan grease fastest yet be kindest to your hands. . . . it is impossible for five different analgesics all to work fast-

er, more effectively than any other, and have the least side effect. It is impossible for ten different cigarettes all to give you more flavor. And so on and on. And it is also impossible, I think, for advertising of this kind eventually to move sensible people to anything but disillusion and disgust.

But it goes further. The public attitudes about advertising cited at the beginning of this book cannot be shrugged off and must not be taken lightly. While some of the criticism is spawned by professional critics who don't understand, or don't want to understand, what advertising really is, while some of it is unwarranted and unfair, a good deal remains to be honestly responded to. The nature of that response, and the promptness of it, are going to influence the future of advertising in this country and around the world. It is clear to me that advertising in the 1980s must fulfill its end of the implicit contract with the consumer more meticulously and more visibly than has ever been attempted in the past. We are being watched.

In 1961 a book entitled *Reality in Advertising* was published. It was written by Rosser Reeves of the Ted Bates advertising agency and achieved great success as advertising books go. The approach espoused by Reeves was, in those pre–Bob Jacoby days, a far cry from what I have been advocating here. In a memo to the organization, Fairfax Cone made this observation about Reeves' book:

> Perhaps it will be most interesting to any of us because, using the same basic principles, we make advertising that is usually as different from the Bates product as day is from night. Bates advertising is built upon what Mr. Reeves calls the Unique Selling Proposition, and he believes in delivering this without subtlety and without concern for anyone's gentler feelings. He also proves that such advertising works.
>
> That it may annoy a great many people, he dismisses as being beside the point.
>
> I don't think this is so.

JOHN O'TOOLE

Dial soap, Clairol, Sunkist, Kleenex, Kotex, Hallmark, Kool-Aid, Kraft candies, Paper-Mate pens, Klear, Raid, Rheingold beer, Dole, etc., all are as successful in their highly competitive fields as any of the Bates-advertised products. All use unique selling propositions that are as carefully developed and tested as those that Rosser Reeves points to in the Bates success. But none uses either jarring or irritating devices, or ugly or questionable illustrations. We undertake to make advertising that is a pleasant intruder, if not, indeed, a welcome one.

This, it seems to me, is the only way that advertising can be done in the public interest. And I don't think anyone else's interest can come first. Whenever it does, advertising is under fire, and properly so.

When one of us in advertising steps out of line, as the Bates company and others did during that era, the rest of us must be just as quick to blow the whistle as Fax was in 1961. We have been polite with one another for too long. We can afford no more of it.

My colleagues in the agency business who concur in general with this point of view—and I believe that includes most—will point out that an agency's influence over the character and quality of a company's advertising is limited. And they are right. If a company insists on advertising that hinges on "weasels" or commercials that are couched in boring formats rather than engaging ideas or television campaigns that penetrate the public consciousness by means of irritating repetition instead of thoughtfulness and humanity, it will get them. The commercials produced by any one agency for all its clients in a year will be far more varied than the commercials run by any one company for all its products. Thus, the advertiser is setting much more visible standards than the agency. This is particularly true of the big soap companies, whose commercials are written and produced by a number of agencies but are all remarkably similar.

Nevertheless, it is the agencies who must, as specialists, provide the dedication and polemic that will render any remaining violations of the implicit contract—and consequently any serious negative attitudes about advertising on the part of the general public—obsolete. I've discussed a number of attitudes and approaches that can foster this goal, but inevitably, as with any sale, we must show that it is in the client's own selfish interests to buy what we're selling. In other words, we must finally document what we all seem to believe: that advertising the prospect likes sells more products than advertising that "bores" him, "annoys" him or "insults his intelligence." We must prove that the way the message is delivered is as critical to making or unmaking a sale as the content.

It may sound simple, but the kind of research necessary to prove such a thesis will be complex, time-consuming and expensive. It will require large samples of consumers and numerous demographic breakouts applied to scores of product categories. It may even be beyond the resources of any one agency, thus necessitating a cooperative effort in a highly competitive industry not noted for working well in unison.

Some beginnings have been made. Rena Bartos of J. Walter Thompson has done a number of studies dealing with women's attitudes about specific commercials directed to them. Probing and analyzing their responses, she has concluded that when women say the commercial insults their intelligence, they mean they don't trust it, they don't believe what the message is telling them. When they say they like a commercial, they mean it's entertaining. When they say it's informative, they mean it has told them what benefits they will derive from using the product. Thus, what these women, at least, are telling us they want from advertising is information in the form of product benefits delivered in a believable and entertaining way.

What manufacturer, after polling his market and finding it demands three things from his product, would refuse to include all of them? Yet when it comes to advertising, some manufacturers still talk about mechanical attributes of the product instead of how it makes life easier or better for the user. Some still couch their information in language and formats that raise de-

227

fenses instead of getting the prospect nodding in agreement. Some still distrust any element in a commercial that appears to entertain, fearing it will dilute the process of persuasion they mistakenly believe to be totally rational. Why? Because as yet we haven't come up with substantive proof that what the prospect is asking for coincides with what is effective in getting him to act upon the message.

I have watched advertising at work for twenty-nine years. All my experience leads me to believe that the characteristics Rena's women request are central to effective commercials. I know product information makes more sales when it's stated in terms of consumer benefits than when it isn't. I saw what happened in the insecticide field when competitors were talking about the exclusive chemicals they used and Raid burst on the market saying, "Raid kills bugs dead." Raid went to first place in six months, and it's still there.

I know that credibility is essential and that a candid message will sell more products than one open to doubt. I saw what happened when we did our first commercial for the Sears Die-Hard battery, in which we actually showed a two-year-old DieHard simultaneously starting five cars with dead batteries. DieHard soon became America's number one replacement battery.

I know entertainment is essential to an effective selling message when it is used to engage the viewer and focus his attention on the benefit. Entertainment performs that function in all of our emotionally moving commercials for Hallmark, a company that sells more greeting cards than all of its competitors combined. For entertainment in advertising is no more limited to humor than it is on the stage or in film. It is anything affective that relevantly illuminates the benefit and fits it into the viewer's life on a human basis.

I know, too, that when advertising embodies these characteristics, it will produce results for the advertiser at a smaller media expenditure than when it does not. I've seen it happen consistently, beginning with Dial soap.

And yet there are some advertisers who, without benefit of similar experiences, mistrust the counsel their own prospects

give. For these remaining holdouts we will have to gather con-
clusive evidence based on actual marketplace performance. I
hope such a study is the subject of the next book on advertising
that appears. I hope I write it.

In the meantime, I'll let the various suggestions put forward
in this book stand as a working plan for improving those bother-
some negative attitudes about a craft I'm quite positive about. If
the plan is put into practice, maybe we'll see articles that
comment on the good side of advertising. Possibly even something like this: "Advertising has changed the way we dress, the
things we eat, our ideas of ventilation, our routine of living, the
very fixtures in our bathrooms. Advertising has contributed
materially to the lengthening of human life." That quote is from
an article entitled "Advertising and Public Health," by the
health commissioner of New York City. It appeared in *Reader's
Digest*. The year was 1922.

Could such an affirmation ever appear today? Not likely. But
perhaps tomorrow. If everyone who practices this craft and
everyone who hires agencies to do it remembers that old admo-
nition of the professional salesman: "To make a sale, you first
have to make a friend."

INDEXES

Index A
SUBJECTS AND PROPER NAMES

SUBJECTS AND PROPER NAMES

Index B
ADVERTISING AGENCIES

INDEX B

Index C
ADVERTISERS AND BRANDS

INDEX C

ADVERTISERS AND BRANDS